Traveling Solo

amplify
an imprint of Amplify Publishing Group

www.amplifypublishinggroup.com

Traveling Solo: A Life Well Lived, A Death Well Planned

To write this book, I relied on memory and interviews, as well as journals, medical records, photos, and calendars. Time is compressed for the sake of narrative flow. In the interest of privacy, some names and identifying details have been changed.

For more information, please contact:
Amplify Publishing, an imprint of Amplify Publishing Group
620 Herndon Parkway, Suite 220
Herndon, VA 20170
info@amplifypublishing.com

Library of Congress Control Number: 2023924574

CPSIA Code: PRV0224A

ISBN-13: 979-8-89138-051-6

Printed in the United States

For my parents, Linda and Bill Williams, who gave me life.
And for my daughters, Isobel and Niulan, who shine as brightly as all the stars in the sky times infinity.

Traveling Solo

A Life Well Lived,
A Death Well Planned

Diana E. Williams

And did you get what
you wanted from this life, even so?
I did.
And what did you want?
To call myself beloved, to feel myself
beloved on the earth.

—Raymond Carver

PREFACE

By the time you read this, I will have followed through on the decision to end my life.

My debilitating, chronic illness was not terminal, and I likely would have lived many more years, long enough, perhaps, to see my two young adult daughters have children of their own.

This book is about why I chose not to.

I never anticipated my story ending like this. Until a few years ago, I saw myself emerging victorious and imagined the synopsis of my book reading something along the lines of:

Diana Williams's inspirational memoir is a tale of triumph. Through sheer determination, she prevailed, and now lives a healthy and vibrant life. Hers was an arduous journey, but she learned to appreciate the gifts inherent in life's challenges and grew as a result of them. She also learned the most important lesson of all: Never, ever give up.

My story, of course, is not about overcoming illness, much less about its redemptive value. But neither is it an account of succumbing to despair. Instead, it is a story of surrender—of accepting that I'd done enough.

While I had the resources to pursue countless treatments and to end my life on my own terms, with the help of a Swiss organization that offers assisted dying for those who are not terminal, this is not the case for millions of others who are suffering.

Although there are currently states that allow medical aid in dying for patients with six months or less to live, there are no legal options for people who do not meet those criteria. Instead, they are left with a choice between continuing to suffer or taking drastic measures.

I wrote this book in the hope that it will evoke compassion for those who endure unending pain and choose to end their lives. I also wrote it as a clarion call for change. Change in our cultural attitudes about death and dying and change in our legislation.

Deciding to end one's life is a personal choice. It should also be a human right.

And with that, I offer you my story.

Diana E. Williams
December 31, 2023

1992 – 1995

When I packed my bags and left New York City for San Francisco, I couldn't have been more ready for a fresh start.

There were many things I wanted to leave in the rearview mirror: the remnants of a short, impulsive marriage; an exorbitant lease that forced me to rent out the bedroom of my apartment and sleep on the couch; a claustrophobic sense of being hemmed in by the gray, steel towers of Manhattan; and a vague feeling that I never belonged in the Big Apple to begin with.

On the heels of my divorce a couple of years earlier, I'd taken a road trip up the West Coast with Margaret, my old college roommate, and had fallen in love with California. The wide-open spaces, the rugged cliffs bordering the vast Pacific, the way the sun cast everything in a lush, golden light. Even the people seemed different—relaxed, unfazed by convention, and more attuned to the things that mattered most to me. I had found the place I wanted to call home.

At the time, I was working in the fundraising department of the Environmental Defense Fund in Manhattan. When I gave my boss notice and told her I was moving to San Francisco, she offered to transfer me to the nonprofit's Oakland office, making the move that much easier.

I knew exactly one person in San Francisco. Arlene was a high school friend who taught yoga at a popular studio. She helped me find a cheap one-bedroom cottage in Russian Hill, and the dog-friendly owner also welcomed Annie, my scruffy six-year-old mutt. The neighborhood offered sweeping views of the Golden Gate Bridge and was crowded with art-filled cafés that roasted their own coffee and hosted game nights. It was a place alive with potential.

I made the cottage my own, including planting pink and orange impatiens in the tiny backyard. Annie curled up at the foot of my bed each night and we drifted off to the low hum of foghorns, waking in the morning to the quaint jangle of cable car bells. One day as I walked Annie, I met Kim, a tall, vivacious Texas transplant with long red hair who lived across the street and was out with her Scottish terrier. We clicked immediately: We were both thirty-two and divorced. Kim and I became fast friends and confidants as she helped me navigate the city's singles scene. We sipped cosmopolitans at elegant bars in the Marina District and took in live music at clubs in North Beach.

I got my fair share of attention from men—I was five foot three and trim, with shoulder-length light brown hair and deep blue eyes—which certainly boosted my self-esteem after my divorce. With a reignited sense of adventure, I took classes in sailing, Zen Buddhism, and yoga. I went running along the shoreline of Crissy Field and spent many happy hours hiking among the orange, poppy-covered hills of the Marin Headlands. I loved being part of the short-lived fad of "tunnel humming," where crowds gathered in abandoned tunnels to hum and feel a mutual vibration and connection. In this eclectic, scenic city, I'd finally found my people.

There was no event more quirkily San Franciscan than the legendary

Bay to Breakers race. More a roving party than a serious footrace, the annual twelve-kilometer event draws thousands of participants, many dressed in outrageous costumes or even running butt naked. Having read about the race for years, in 1994 I signed up to run with two friends.

One brisk morning in late May, we joined throngs of runners at the Embarcadero, the boulevard that runs along the city's eastern waterfront. Although the day was shrouded in chilly fog, the persistent California sun had begun to burn a hole in the low clouds. All around us, people laughed and hopped from one leg to the other, trying to warm up. When a siren sounded, we surged forward en masse, cheered on by crowds lining the sidewalks and leaning out of windows.

After I'd run about a mile, a wave of exhaustion hit me. I was in good running shape, but I suddenly felt weighed down, as if I were dragging an invisible anchor.

Am I coming down with the flu?

Pushing through the fatigue was impossible. I slowed to a walk and told my friends to forge ahead. "I'm so sorry, you guys," I panted. "I don't know what's wrong." They graciously stayed with me, but by the time we reached the finish line at Ocean Beach, on San Francisco's western edge, I was utterly spent. Instead of the endorphin high that running normally gave me, I had a pounding headache.

As other runners ducked into bars to celebrate completing the race, I hauled myself home and slept for twelve hours straight. I woke up refreshed but a bit spooked.

What the hell was that?

Little did I know I'd spend the next three decades running—chasing an elusive finish line that never seemed to come.

I shrugged off the episode until a few months later, when my body betrayed me again, this time on a much-needed vacation from a grueling work schedule: a scuba-diving trip to Cozumel, Mexico. After a day of exploring underwater reefs teeming with technicolor fish, I'd joined the other divers for tacos and margaritas. But later that night, I woke up bathed in sweat. The budget hotel room didn't have air conditioning, and the lively breeze off the ocean wasn't enough to cool me down. Drenching sweats kept me awake for the next four nights and persisted after I returned home, despite the notoriously cool San Francisco night air.

My general practitioner, a pleasant man in his forties named Dr. Whittaker, suspected that I'd picked up a bacterial infection and prescribed an antibiotic. But the medicine did nothing and the night sweats continued, now accompanied by the same whole-body exhaustion I'd felt during the race. Over the following months, the symptoms came and went. Some weeks I was fine, but then fatigue blindsided me like a recurring bad dream.

When I returned to Dr. Whittaker, he reviewed my chart and pushed back his chair to fix me with a serious look. "Well," he said in a gravelly voice. "It could very well be perimenopause."

I winced. I was only thirty-five.

"I'm sorry, what?"

He explained that some women go through menopause early, and that my hot flashes and fatigue were two classic signs. I was devastated. I'd always wanted to become a mother and now he was telling me that my ovaries were shutting down?

Dr. Whittaker ordered a blood panel to check my hormone levels, and I spent an anxious week waiting for the results. Suddenly, all I could think about was having a baby. When the tests showed that my hormone levels were normal, I breathed a sigh of relief.

But I continued to worry about my mysterious symptoms. My

neighbor recommended her naturopath, so I booked an appointment even though my insurance didn't cover the services. I was hopeful that alternative medicine could identify the problem, since mainstream medicine was drawing a blank.

Dr. DuBrow's office was just a few blocks from my apartment. After being buzzed through a narrow door squeezed between a furniture store and coffee shop, I climbed a long flight of stairs and entered the light-filled space of a converted living room. I sank into a plush armchair as Dr. DuBrow, a thirty-something woman with oversized glasses, handed me a cup of herbal tea.

After reviewing my symptoms, she nodded knowingly. "I'm guessing you have adrenal fatigue."

In 1995, adrenal fatigue was the diagnosis *du jour*. The adrenal glands, located above the kidneys, produce several hormones, including cortisol. Stress causes the adrenal glands to release bursts of cortisol into the bloodstream, which jacks up the heart rate, prompting the fight-or-flight response that has kept humans alive for millennia.

Adrenal fatigue theorized that prolonged stress drains the adrenals of cortisol, leading to a host of vague symptoms. Exhausted? *Must be adrenal fatigue.* Can't sleep? *Adrenal fatigue.* Feeling sad? *Adrenal fatigue.* Body aches? Headaches? Loss of appetite? *Adrenal fatigue.* Later, I learned that adrenal fatigue isn't an accepted medical diagnosis.

Dr. DuBrow had me spit into a small vial so she could test my cortisol levels. When the results came back, she officially diagnosed me with—of course—adrenal fatigue. She seemed a lot more confident in her diagnosis than Dr. Whittaker had in his.

Thank God for a straightforward answer.

She recommended getting more sleep and laying off sugar. More sleep wasn't a problem, but I found the sugar restriction challenging; I had a habit of scarfing down a small bag of M&Ms most nights after dinner. She also prescribed ashwagandha, an anti-stress supplement derived from an African shrub, as well as adrenal capsules to boost my energy. I tried not to fixate on the fact that the adrenal capsules were made from desiccated cow adrenal glands and happily handed over my money, eager to start the treatment that would set me straight again.

We put our faith in doctors, who spend years studying the human body and how to cure it, and then we get well. We trust doctors to have all the answers to make us better. Because that's the way it works, right?

Not always. I just didn't know it yet.

1996 – 1999

The shrub and dried bovine supplements appeared to work, and after a couple of months I stopped taking them. I felt more energetic and took up running and yoga again.

I also began to dip a toe back into the dating scene. At the time, San Francisco was ground zero for the dot-com boom and teemed with young, single men. Although I was eager for romance, I still smarted from my divorce and worried about making another misstep.

One night over drinks, as my neighbor Kim and I discussed our short first marriages, she said that her therapist had helped her learn to make better choices in men. She jotted down the woman's name on a napkin.

The first time I met with Elizabeth, an elegant woman in her mid-forties with shoulder-length blonde hair, I knew I was in good hands. She exuded a warmth that put me at ease and asked gently probing questions to help me understand what I hoped for in a potential mate.

Elizabeth suggested I create a list of qualities I desired. The top three: (1) He must have a good relationship with his mother, (2) he must be a good listener, and (3) he must love dogs.

After a year of dating only incompatible men, I started to give up hope that I'd ever marry again or become a mother. A neighbor, a single woman in her early forties, had recently adopted a toddler girl from China. When I saw her walking with her daughter, the two of them holding hands and laughing, I felt a pang of longing. I'd always known I wanted to be a mother; even more, I wanted to be a mother to a daughter. My neighbor referred me to Adopt International and I began the process of applying to become a single mom, filling out paperwork and scheduling a home study.

But then, one fine Saturday afternoon, Bob strolled into my life—or, rather, into my hot hatha yoga class. As usual, I was late, and the 104-degree room was packed with lithe, sweaty yogis. Spotting a free space next to one of the few men, I picked my way toward it and unfurled my mat.

As Arlene led us through a series of poses, I showed off a little—easily contorting my flexible body into most of them—and stealing glances at the handsome, thirty-something man next to me. He stood tall and wiry in Tree Pose, and he had a mop of dark hair and a superhero jawline. I'd later learn that he'd once appeared in *GQ* magazine as a chin model for expensive ties.

I grew shy when the class ended, avoiding eye contact as I rolled up my mat. Later, I peppered Arlene with questions.

"Bob?" she answered. "He seems like a great guy!"

The next Saturday I followed her down a crowded hallway to where he sat on a bench tying his shoes. He rose as she introduced us, towering over me and gazing into my face with piercing blue eyes. I swooned a bit.

At the end of the next class, Bob invited me to a party at his apartment. I enlisted a friend as my wingwoman and spent an afternoon trying on different outfits, wanting to look hot but not as if I tried too hard. When we arrived at Bob's studio, we found it packed—mostly with women. *Christ. I guess I'm not the only one who thinks he's cute.* I glanced around the confined space, trying to get a better sense of him. The first thing I noticed was that he'd converted his closet into an office, removing the door and wedging in a desk and large monitor. Cables secured with electrical tape snaked across the floor.

After watching him chat with other women out of the corner of my eye for twenty minutes, I told my friend I wanted to leave. It was then that he walked over. "You made it!" he said, kissing me on the cheek and handing us both a glass of wine.

Another guest pulled him away and we slipped out. With all that competition, I didn't expect to hear from him again. When he called a few days later to invite me to coffee, I felt giddy. We met at a local roastery, ordered our drinks, and sank into armchairs to talk. I was eager to push past his polished exterior and get to know him. But as we chatted, he seemed distracted and kept glancing at his watch.

"I'm so sorry, Diana," he said, looking again at his wrist. "I hate to cut this short, but I've got a lot of balls in the air."

Bob explained that he'd just launched a marketing business catering to tech companies and was facing several looming deadlines. He left his half-finished cappuccino on the table and rushed off. I couldn't help but feel a little rejected.

"Well, that was a bust," I told Kim when she called to get the skinny.

But a few weeks later he called again, this time to invite me to the ballet. I donned a black satin dress with a plunging neckline. Bob, dressed in a dark suit, looked irresistibly debonair. At the elegant marble theater, we settled into red velvet seats, and Bob reached for my hand as we watched a gorgeous production of Balanchine's *Ballo della Regina*. When he dropped me off at my cottage later that night, we shared our first kiss.

Despite our promising start, we continued to dance around each other for the next several months. Both of us were skittish; Bob had also been heartbroken by the end of a long-term relationship.

I had a magnificent hunch about him, though. We got to know each other on long walks through San Francisco, dinners out and dinners in, and I began to let my guard down. How could I not? For starters, he met the top requirements on my "must-have" list: He was attentive to his mother, he was incredibly fond of Annie, and he was a good listener. He was also eager to become a father. I let myself fall in love.

By Valentine's Day 1997, we'd been dating for a little over a year. Bob invited me over that evening, and when I arrived, I found a trail of votive candles lining the stairs that led up to his apartment. I followed them through his open door, where a magical scene awaited: Within a circle of twinkling votives lay an open box holding a diamond ring. As I gazed down at it, Bob rounded the corner and took my hands in his.

"Diana, will you marry me?" His voice was thick with emotion. I nodded, unable to speak. Tears filled my eyes.

Seven months later, on September 6, we were married in the elegant gardens of the Olema Inn in Pt. Reyes, an hour north of San Francisco. Kim was my maid of honor, Elizabeth served as our officiant, and our families flew in, mine from the East Coast and his from the Midwest.

The next day, Bob and I flew to Kaua'i. We hiked the eight-mile Hanakāpī'ai trail on the Nāpali Coast, snorkeled on the reef, and slept off the stress of planning a wedding, curled up together and lulled to sleep by the sound of crashing waves.

Throughout our courtship and early marriage, I'd all but forgotten the mysterious ailments that had besieged me a few years earlier. Although I was occasionally fatigued, I chalked it up to work stress or wedding planning—nothing a good night's sleep wouldn't remedy.

Given our ages (I was thirty-eight and Bob was forty), we were eager to start a family. After six months of trying, however, we booked a consultation at a fertility clinic.

Dr. Floyd, a Southerner who favored bow ties and wore thick glasses that magnified his eyes, was direct. "Well," he drawled, "you two aren't getting any younger. It's time to fish or cut bait."

He recommended starting in vitro fertilization (IVF) but warned us that the success rate for women my age was just 35 percent. We decided to take the chance.

My life soon revolved around doctors' appointments, blood tests, hormone injections, and ultrasounds. The injections were self-administered and followed a complicated schedule. Perched on the side of the tub, I'd pinch my belly fat and jab it with a needle, then rub it in for good measure. My abdomen soon became an abstract map of yellow-green bruises—proof, I hoped, that the hormones were working their magic.

But they also gave me headaches and hot flashes, which Dr. Floyd said were common side effects of fertility treatment. The mental and physical stress of bearing the brunt of our attempts to start a family, combined with escalating conflicts with a new boss, prompted me to quit my job. It was a relief. Now I could put all my energy into trying to get pregnant.

After three weeks of injections, the doctor removed eggs from my ovaries and mixed them with Bob's sperm, giving us five viable embryos. Bob held my hand as Dr. Floyd inserted them into my uterus, with the hope that one would survive. On the ultrasound monitor, the embryos looked like stars shooting across a black sky.

How amazing that modern medicine can give me a baby!

I was thrilled when we found out that one of the embryos had implanted, and I rushed to the neighborhood bookstore to buy *What to Expect When You're Expecting*. I also bought an overpriced green polka dot onesie at a children's boutique on Union Street. This was, I thought, the beginning of a new life.

My luck seemed to continue, as I had no morning sickness. But during an ultrasound a few weeks later, we learned that I'd miscarried. I was crushed. Bob hugged me as we cried together. "It's okay," he assured me. "We'll try again."

I went through another grueling round of IVF. Once again, I had headaches and hot flashes, and I worried about the repercussions of taking so many hormones. But I comforted myself with the belief that someday soon I would hold my own baby. I just had to stay the course.

This time eight eggs were removed from my ovaries, and we ended up with six viable embryos. But the day before the embryo transfer, the clinic called with devastating news: The incubator had overheated and none of our embryos had survived. Bob and I were as angry as we were grief-stricken. I couldn't help but think that one of them could have been our child.

After much negotiation, the clinic agreed to cover the cost of the next procedure but insisted that we pay for the expensive hormones—including a new one that was supposed to increase my ability to become pregnant. I steeled myself for a third round of IVF.

Yet another round of embryos was inserted into my womb, and a few weeks later one of the clinic's doctors called. "Congratulations! You're pregnant!"

But I didn't feel pregnant. None of the signs I'd had the first time—the tender breasts and increased appetite—were there. Not quite convinced, I called Dr. Floyd to verify the results. After apologizing profusely, he confirmed that his colleague had misinterpreted the lab report; the new hormone had given a false positive.

Once again, our elation was dashed. Bob and I discussed finding a new fertility clinic, but the best ones had long wait lists. We had no time to lose.

Meanwhile, babies seemed to be everywhere, a constant reminder of my inability to create one. My heart constricted whenever a stroller wheeled by with a sleeping infant or a friend announced that she was pregnant. The baby-toting club was one I desperately wanted to join, and I felt out of control. This would not be the last time modern medicine would leave me with such a feeling.

After much soul-searching, we decided to attempt one last round of IVF. We'd nearly drained our savings, so this would be our Hail Mary pass. The physical stress on my body was arduous, but the emotional roller coaster of hope and loss was far worse.

Our Hail Mary paid off. I was pregnant! For the next nine months, I lived in a state of joy tempered with disbelief, worried that I'd somehow jinx it. Even as my belly stretched the waistband of my maternity pants, I wasn't convinced that our baby was beyond danger. I was also extremely fatigued, but my obstetrician told me that was probably due to my "advanced maternal age." It never occurred to me that what I was experiencing might be related to what had felled me during the Bay to Breakers race a few years earlier.

By mid-July 1998, I was a week overdue and impatient to meet our baby, who, to my delight, was a girl. We booked a couple of nights at a funky inn at Stinson Beach, hoping that long walks along the shore might kick things into gear. I had discovered Stinson Beach—a stunning three-mile crescent of white sand just north of the city—shortly after moving to San Francisco. I often made the forty-five-minute drive over the Golden Gate Bridge with Annie, who loved to romp in the surf.

After checking in at the hotel, I looped my arm through Bob's and waddled down to the beach to watch the sunset. As we slowly made our way past the lingering sunbathers, I found a heart-shaped rock and slipped it into my pocket, a keepsake for our baby girl. We were almost-but-not-quite-yet parents and acutely aware that the quiet routines of couplehood would end when we became three.

That night, I woke up with a pinching sensation in my lower pelvis. When I heaved myself out of bed and stood, warm fluid gushed down my leg.

"Oh my God! Bob!" I called out, feeling equal parts terrified and excited.

Bob jumped up and hugged me before gathering our bags and bundling me into the car. We sped along the narrow, curvy coastal road of Route 1 toward the hospital in San Francisco, where I was wheeled to Labor and Delivery.

I'd called my parents on the way, and they flew in from the East Coast eleven hours later, eager to be in the delivery room to welcome their first grandchild. I was wearing my mother's pearl necklace. My father had given it to her as a wedding gift, telling her that he wanted their first child to be a girl. And it was: me. When my mom learned we were having problems conceiving, she'd given me the necklace as a good luck charm, with the thought that someday I'd bequeath those same pearls to my own daughter.

After a relatively easy labor, my baby slid into the world, prune-faced and wailing. As soon as a nurse placed her in my arms, instead of bursting into tears of joy, as I'd imagined I would, I checked the color of her eyes. They looked very dark—not blue like Bob's and my eyes. I panicked, worried that the clinic had created one last fiasco by mixing up our embryos with another family's. It was known to happen.

"Are her eyes brown?" I asked the nurse as she scribbled in my chart.

She glanced at the baby before turning back to her notes. "Sometimes it's hard to tell with newborns," she said.

I continued to scrutinize every inch of my baby, peering at her face, her tiny ears, her little hands. Then I noticed it: her pinky fingers curved ever so slightly inward—the familiar curve I knew from the pinkies of my grandmother and father.

Ah, yes, she was our baby.

As we'd considered names months earlier, I'd thought about my own. My parents were going to name me either Diana or Elisa. They couldn't decide between the two, however, so my father asked the sixteen-year-old boys in his English class to vote. Diana won by a landslide.

In grade school, I'd looked up "Diana" in the World Book Encyclopedia and learned that she was the Roman goddess of fertility, the hunt, and the moon—in other words, she was a powerful woman. Bob and I decided to pass down the lunar symbolism to our daughter as well. We named her Isobel, spelled with an "o," so that she would hold the shape of the moon in her name. Every night, I'd carry her down our apartment hallway past three black-and-white photos of the full moon near Pt. Reyes, where Bob and I were married, saying, "Goodnight, Mrs. Moon."

For the first months of Isobel's life, I lived in the blur of new motherhood, sleep-deprived but completely enamored of the tiny creature my body had created. My schedule revolved around breastfeeding and diaper changes and naps, and I melted every time she offered me a toothless grin.

But when she was four months old, postpartum depression ambushed me. The constant infant care I'd initially embraced was now onerous; I was irritable, tearful, and exhausted. The mere thought of carrying Isobel and her stroller down the apartment steps to the park was overwhelming.

I reminded myself to be grateful for the miracle of her life and continued to play the part of Super Mom, breastfeeding on demand and then, when she started eating solids, making her food from organic produce I'd buy at the farmer's market. One day, as I pureed beets, the top of the blender flew off and red pulp spattered across the ceiling, walls, and me. It looked like a murder scene.

Great, now I have to clean this up, too.

Isobel, who was buckled in her highchair, began to wail with hunger, and I slumped to the floor and wailed along with her.

This felt like more than just "the baby blues," so I went to see Dr. Whittaker. After my divorce, I'd taken Prozac to help me through a rough emotional patch. Now Dr. Whittaker recommended I take it again, but with the caveat that I'd have to stop nursing Isobel. That gave me pause. In my mom's circles, there was tremendous pressure to breastfeed for as long as possible to maximize the immunity and bonding benefits. My intention had been to nurse Isobel, affectionately known as Izzy, until her first birthday. But after several days mulling it over, I realized that to be the mother she needed, I had to take charge of my emotional health. I needed to help myself before I could help my child.

It took a few weeks, but the Prozac worked. Once again, I took delight in the small joys of motherhood. I was still exhausted much of the time, but weren't all new parents?

Looking back, however, I realize that what I'd experienced wasn't normal new-parent fatigue. It was an early warning sign of what would develop, slowly but relentlessly, into an overwhelming health issue that would derail my life.

2000 – 2001

Izzy was now a toddler, and we'd outgrown our San Francisco apartment. Bob's marketing business was thriving, and we were able to buy a home in Mill Valley, a small town nestled at the base of Mt. Tamalpais, just an eight-mile drive over the Golden Gate Bridge from San Francisco. Mill Valley had a small-town feel, complete with a downtown square where people gathered to socialize over coffee and dance to live music on Sunday evenings.

One Friday shortly after we'd moved, I drove Izzy to preschool and returned home to my desk. I'd started a business called FlexMoms.com, an online platform to help mothers find part-time, flexible work. I'd recruited four friends, and we brainstormed ideas for content and website design. It was still very much in the start-up phase; nobody was getting paid, but we were hoping, in those heady dot-com days, to find venture capital funding. If Pets.com could make it, why couldn't we?

As I sipped a second cup of coffee and checked my inbox, I noticed that the waistband of my jeans felt uncomfortably tight. *Damn, I've gotta lay off the ice cream.*

I changed into yoga pants and returned to my desk, but the strange feeling persisted. The left side of my torso was numb and weirdly heavy—the kind of feeling you get in your cheek as the novocaine wears off after dental work. Over the next two days, the numbness spread down my left leg, all the way to my toes. It was a pins-and-needles, foot-falling-asleep sensation. I wondered if it was from slouching at my desk for too many hours at a time. I started taking breaks throughout the day, getting up and moving around every hour or so. But the numbness continued and was soon accompanied by extreme fatigue more severe than anything I'd ever experienced, even after Isobel was born.

On the fourth day, no amount of coffee could help me fight my way through the exhaustion, so I called Bob and asked him to pick up Izzy and grab dinner on his way home. I crawled into bed around 3 p.m. and slept until the next morning. But the bizarre symptoms lingered.

Was it a pinched nerve? Burnout from working too much? A virus?

Just as I hadn't considered there might be a link between my near-collapse during the Bay to Breakers run, the night sweats I'd suffered in Mexico, and my excessive pregnancy fatigue, I didn't make the connection this time either. I'd put all that behind me.

I stayed in bed the entire weekend. After months of feeling frazzled as we worked to launch FlexMoms.com, I relished the time to myself. Tucked under my down comforter and between long naps, I watched *When Harry Met Sally* and ate peanut M&Ms. Bob fussed over me, bringing trays of food, and Izzy slipped get-well cards drawn with scented markers under my pillow.

When I hadn't improved by Monday, I called Dr. Whittaker, who was alarmed enough by my symptoms to refer me to the neurology clinic of a San Francisco hospital. I figured it would probably turn out to be nothing more than a pinched nerve, but Bob encouraged me to go. Better safe than sorry.

A few days later, Bob and I headed into the city for the appointment. The neurologist, a harried man with a shock of white hair, conducted a series of tests. He analyzed my gait as I walked down the hallway, evaluated my reflexes by stroking the soles of my feet with a pencil and tapping just below my kneecap with a rubber hammer, checked the ability of my eyes to focus by having me track his finger, and assessed the strength of my grip as I squeezed his hand.

Afterward, he sat behind his desk and motioned for Bob and me to sit across from him. He frowned.

"Your reflexes look fine, but I'm concerned about the numbness and fatigue," he said. "We need to rule out multiple sclerosis."

I sank back into my chair and Bob grabbed my hand.

The neurologist suggested more tests—immediately. The next morning, as Bob camped out in the waiting room with his laptop, I followed the nurse to an examination room, where I donned a hospital gown. As I lay on my side, the doctor inserted a long needle into my spine to aspirate cerebrospinal fluid. His nurse then accompanied me to another wing of the hospital for an MRI scan of my brain.

For the first time, I was worried.

When the results came in a week later, I was in the garden. It was early summer, and I'd dragged myself outside to plant Sun Gold cherry tomato seedlings, a variety that thrives in foggy Marin summers. My symptoms hadn't let up, but I knew fresh air and a distraction would be good for me. I'd jammed my cell phone into my back pocket, turning the volume all the way up so I wouldn't miss a call.

When my phone rang, I jumped, startled by the sound.

My neurologist got straight to the point. "The test results of your spinal tap are consistent with multiple sclerosis. When the immune system attacks your central nervous system, it shows up as plaque, which appears as white spots on the MRI."

I grabbed the flimsy tomato cage to steady myself, wobbling in the afternoon stillness.

"You'll need to make an appointment with Dr. Singh, our MS specialist, as soon as you can. I'll forward your records to him. I'm sorry for the not-so-good news."

Not-so-good news?

I sank to my knees on the muddy ground and stared at the crooked row of baby tomato plants. I felt like I was going to throw up.

I knew multiple sclerosis (MS) was a devastating and incurable disease, but that's all I knew. I'd avoided reading about it because I didn't want to scare myself, but now I went inside, pushed aside the unwashed breakfast dishes on the kitchen table, and opened my laptop. The National Multiple Sclerosis Society's website informed me that "damage to myelin, the protective layer insulating wire-like nerve fibers, disrupts signals to and from the brain, causing unpredictable symptoms such as numbness, tingling, mood changes, memory problems, pain, fatigue, blindness, and/or paralysis."

Blindness? Paralysis?

I slapped my laptop shut and walked around the house, hugging myself and crying, trying not to wake Isobel from her nap.

I waited until Bob came home to break the news. I'd given Isobel a new can of pink Play-Doh to distract her as I made supper, and she sat cross-legged in front of the refrigerator, rolling it into pea-sized balls.

Bob set his briefcase on the sofa and walked into the kitchen, his smile evaporating when he saw my stricken face.

"The doctor says I have MS," I blurted. He gathered me into his arms, and I cried into his shoulder. There was nothing to say; I just needed to be held.

"We'll get through this," he said.

We were anxious to discuss treatment options with the specialist as soon as possible. But when I called Dr. Singh's office the next morning, the receptionist told me he didn't have an opening for another two months.

"I can't wait that long," I told her, desperation pinching my voice. "My body's going numb, and I can barely get out of bed. Please, is there *anything* you can do?"

"If you're really sick, you should go to the emergency room," she replied offhandedly.

Oh, for the love of God.

"Can you at least put me on the cancellation list?" I asked, my voice rising.

"We don't really have one," she said. "People usually keep their appointments."

I tried to swallow my sobs, but she could hear me. I didn't care.

"Listen," she whispered, when I finally took a deep, ragged breath, "I'm here most mornings by 8 a.m. Call me before 8:15, and I'll let you know if anyone cancels. But I may only be able to give you an hour's notice. Can you do that?"

"Yes," I whispered back. "Thank you!"

Bob set an alarm to call the clinic every morning while I slept. On the tenth morning, he nabbed an appointment.

After dropping Izzy at preschool, we drove to San Francisco, arriving at the clinic early. In the waiting room, I took in the brochures lying on the table before us—*Mental Health in MS Patients. Seizure Control in MS Patients. Paralysis in MS Patients*—before quickly averting my eyes.

Dr. Singh, a short man with large brown eyes, gave me another physical exam. As he held up my left hand, he noticed a slight tremor in my ring finger and pinkie, which he noted in my chart.

Throughout the exam, I bombarded him with questions: "How did I get this?" "Will I go blind?" "Will my daughter inherit this from me?"

"We really don't know," was his repeated answer. His flat delivery irritated me. "After five years, we should have a pretty good idea of your situation," he said. "You'll need an annual MRI to see if your brain and spinal cord show more 'plaquing'—which would mean the MS is progressing."

I left his office with a prescription for Copaxone, whose active ingredient was a synthetic protein that blocked myelin-damaging T-cells and controlled the immune response. The medication had to be injected three times a week, and a few days later, a company representative came to the house to show me how to do it myself.

I welcomed her inside, and she looked around expectantly. "When will your husband be joining us?" she asked. She was in her forties and sported a navy blazer and thick blue eyeliner.

"I'll be doing the injections myself," I said. "I did IVF, so it's pretty familiar territory."

She gave me a sad look and shook her head. "But how will you inject yourself when you're too disabled to hold the needle?"

I held her gaze, trying to figure out if she was clueless or being deliberately cruel. Either way, I wasn't ready to face a future she seemed insistent on shoving in my face. She offered a tight smile that I suppose was meant to be sympathetic.

"Just tell me what to do," I said through my teeth.

The Copaxone had to be stored in the refrigerator, she explained, but brought to room temperature before use; injecting it cold would be painful. She handed me an illustration of a human figure with numbers marking injection sites on the abdomen, thighs, hips, and back of the arms. She told me to rotate through the seven injection sites.

Over my objections, she insisted on a demonstration, pinching my thigh and pretending to jab it. "After you remove the needle, apply pressure, like this," she said, pressing my leg with cold fingers.

I fought the urge to smack her hand away. I hated this woman and her icy certainty that I would become an invalid. I wanted her to get away from me, to get out of my house.

After she left, I bolted the door.

2002 – 2005

For the next two years, I waited for the other shoe to drop. I waited for weakness, changes in vision, difficulty walking. For creeping, debilitating paralysis. But thankfully, none of that happened; the Copaxone appeared to be working, and my annual MRIs looked good. While the doctor could see the original plaquing, there was no evidence of further damage to my brain or spinal cord. Aside from the mysterious numbness on the left side of my body that never went away, and occasional bouts of exhaustion, I was stable.

It seemed like the right time to have a second child. Bob and I both grew up with siblings we were close to and wanted Isobel to have that close relationship, too. But we had no interest in going through the rigors or expense of IVF again. I'd told Bob about my San Francisco neighbor who'd adopted a girl from China, and he knew of my plans to use the same adoption agency to become a single mom had he not appeared in my life. We clicked through Adopt International's website together, feeling hopeful and excited as we studied a photo of a group of children at one of the orphanages.

"Let's do it!" we agreed. We sent the email form to start the process.

After a year of filling out mountains of paperwork and several nerve-racking home visits, the agency approved our application, and we were put on a waiting list with a Chinese orphanage. We decided it was time to give Izzy, who was four, the good news.

"Izzy, I have a question for you," I said one morning as I crouched on her bedroom floor, pulling a shirt over her curly blonde head. "How would you feel about having a sister?"

Her big blue eyes widened. "A sister?"

"Yes. What do you think?"

She nodded enthusiastically, then scrunched her face in confusion.

"Mama, am I the big sister or the little sister?" Her face grew serious. "I think I should be the big sister."

I pulled her into my arms, laughing. "You will be the best big sister ever!"

Several months later, a FedEx package arrived with a letter and a wallet-sized photograph of a fifteen-month-old baby swaddled in a thick sweater that was several sizes too big. A corona of jet-black hair framed her plump, rosy cheeks. She'd been abandoned on a bridge in Nanchang, the capital of Jiangxi province, the letter said, and taken to a local orphanage. Her name was Niulan, but she was called by her nickname, Nunu.

Seeing her face, I was overcome with excitement and joy. Responsibility, too. Her life was now in our hands.

Who is this little person who will soon call me Mom?

We were eager to bring her home as soon as possible. I rushed out to buy a crib and pink-striped curtains and bedding, as well as a toddler-height shelf for toys. Isobel donated a few of her beloved stuffed animals, which she carefully arranged on the shelf.

In early March of 2003, my parents flew out to stay with Izzy while Bob and I traveled to Nanchang. It would be a brief trip, but our oversized suitcases were jammed. I'd packed everything I could imagine our new daughter might need, from toys to clothing to a nasal syringe.

We were going stir-crazy as we waited for the orphanage workers to bring Nunu to our hotel. They were hours late. We paced the room, folded and refolded Nunu's clothes, and tried to decipher the soap opera on the TV. Finally, in the early evening, there was a knock at the door, and I dashed to open it, catching my hip on the corner of a dresser. In the doorway were a translator, two women from the orphanage, and Nunu—asleep in her caretaker's arms. Just as in the photo, she was wrapped in layers of clothing and looked like a little Michelin Man. I reached for her, but the woman holding her brushed past me and lowered Nunu into the crib the hotel had provided. "The baby will sleep in the crib," the translator told us. "She will wake in the morning to see you."

"I can't wait for morning," I said. I'd been imagining this moment for over a year. She was my baby; I had to hold her. The caretaker frowned but brought her over to me. I took Nunu into my arms, nuzzling the top of her head and inhaling her scent. *My daughter*, I whispered into the brown whorl of her tiny ear.

She started to squirm, then woke and stared wide-eyed into my face. What a strange sight I must have been—pale-skinned, light hair, blue eyes. Her face fell into a frown, and she started to bawl. The caretaker handed me a bottle of formula, and after she left, I sat cross-legged on the floor, Bob beside me, feeding and rocking her. We gazed at her beautiful face, and when she fell asleep, Bob carried her to the crib, where she slept on her back with her arms stretched over her head—a sleep position she retained well into her teenage years.

The next morning when she woke, we brought her into our bed. It didn't take her long to get over the shock of our unfamiliar faces, and she began jumping on the bed and giggling. We spoke to her in English, though her quizzical looks told us she had no idea what we were saying. Nor, of course, did we understand the babbling sounds she made. But Bob and I were relieved to see that our new daughter had such a confident, easy-going disposition.

Nunu had arrived wearing traditional split-bottom pants called *kaidangku*, which Chinese toddlers often wore instead of diapers, and which made it easier to go potty on command—on a toilet, in the grass, or even when held over a trash can. We laughed as Nunu toddled around with her little bottom showing. But since we didn't know how the system worked or whether she'd even mastered it, we put a diaper on her, which she probably found odd, uncomfortable, and more than a little disgusting.

During the sixteen-hour flight home, she was too busy taking in her surroundings to sleep. What a momentous transition it must have been for her, going from familiar sights, sounds, and smells to being in an airplane bouncing through the sky, held by two strangers who didn't speak her language. She crawled between my lap and Bob's and pressed her face to the window—cooing and patting the glass—and toddled down the aisle holding my hand, stopping at each row to tilt her face and smile up at the passengers. She finally settled into a deep sleep just as we landed, her head a dead weight on Bob's shoulder.

My parents and Isobel met us in baggage claim with a hand-painted sign: "Welcome Home, Nunu!" Izzy ran over to the stroller and gently kissed Nunu's cheek. By the time we carried her into the house, she was wide awake again and dashed from room to room. She batted at the bouquet of pastel balloons my parents had bought for her, then plopped down on the floor with Izzy to play with her new toys.

I often looked around the dinner table with deep gratitude as I considered the synchronicity that made our family possible. Bob and I happened to show up for the same yoga class. Our DNA combined in just the right way to create Isobel. And of all the children in the world, it was this bright, happy child who came into our lives.

I was reminded of the Chinese proverb: "An invisible red thread connects those who are destined to meet regardless of time, place, or circumstance. The thread may stretch or tangle but will never break."

Looking back, those years as a young family feel even more precious because, though I didn't know it at the time, my carefree days were numbered.

In the winter of 2004, almost a year after we brought Nunu home, I caught a bad cold that devolved into a sinus infection. Three months later, despite multiple rounds of antibiotics, the pain and pressure persisted. Dr. Whittaker sent me to the hospital for an X-ray to see if there was a blockage of some sort. The X-ray came back negative, but I felt as though I had the flu—fatigue, nausea, chills, headaches, and the night sweats I'd experienced during my 1995 scuba diving trip in Mexico. This cluster of symptoms would dog me for the rest of my life, erupting sporadically, sometimes separately, and sometimes all at once.

In the many years of dealing with this illness, it's become clear that a single, "correct" diagnosis simply doesn't exist. My symptoms have remained a mystery, and treatment has been elusive.

In these ways, there are many parallels to long COVID, another medical enigma. As Georgia Lupi, who suffers with long COVID, wrote in the *New York Times* just a few weeks before my death, "chronic illness, stretching over months and years, has a way of picking apart your mind and breaking your heart. It is a constant deluge of pain that slowly strips you of everything you used to be by taking away everything you used to do—daily exercise, going out more nights than not, seeing friends, attending concerts, traveling the world and, eventually, laughter, smiles and the ability to imagine a future without harsh physical limits."

She concludes by noting, "Even if my body, from the outside, resembles the old me, long COVID has rewritten my core personhood on a cellular level."

The exhaustion was the most difficult aspect of my condition. It wasn't an I-just-hiked-twenty-miles tired or an I-didn't-sleep-last-night tired. It was an alarming, energy-sapping, "something's wrong" tired.

Dr. Whittaker was convinced I didn't have the flu, but thought the symptoms were a lingering effect of the sinus infection or another low-grade infection. They continued intermittently for several more months before slowly fading away on their own.

After I regained my stamina, I toyed with the idea of rebooting FlexMoms.com, but my former partners had moved on to other work, and I didn't want to start from scratch with a whole new crew. Now that Isobel was in kindergarten and Nunu in preschool, I had more free time and was restless. I wanted to get out of the house but didn't want to commit to a full-time job while the girls were so young.

I recalled seeing a flyer at the community center calling for hospice volunteers for Marin General Hospital. Volunteering would offer a great way to feel useful for a few hours a week.

After a couple of weeks of training, I became a "Spiritual Care Provider." On my first day, I felt rather official wearing a pager on my waistband that summoned me to the rooms of hospice patients in need of company. I still felt insecure about my ability to help, but my supervisor assured me things would get easier.

One of the first people I sat with was a San Quentin State Prison inmate. Marin General was just a few miles from the prison and offered more sophisticated healthcare than the prison infirmary. I didn't know the medical reasons that brought the man to the hospital, but the intervention had clearly failed, and he was fading fast.

When I entered his room, a uniformed San Quentin guard gave me a curt nod and stepped into the hallway, leaving the door ajar. I looked across the room, taking in the prisoner's massive, muscle-bound body. He was lying on his back, his head turned away from me. Both of his wrists were handcuffed to the bed railing; I assumed he was violent and worried for my safety.

What the hell am I doing here?

Later, I'd learn that all prisoners were cuffed to their beds, regardless of their offense or the severity of their health issues. It was simply protocol.

I walked to the far side of the bed and quietly pulled a chair up beside him. He looked to be in his forties. A cobweb prison tattoo laced his neck under his gown. I had a sudden, irrational fear that he'd wake up and grab me, despite the handcuffs and the guard standing just ten feet away, but after a few minutes, I calmed down. His eyes were closed, and he was breathing irregularly, taking great gulps of air and then appearing not to breathe at all. It was clear he was close to the end.

During training, I'd done rounds with the program director, who modeled how to stay present with the dying. But I couldn't help my thoughts from racing as I sat in that quiet room, everything from wondering what crimes the man had committed, to what I wanted for lunch, to when I was supposed to pick up Nunu from her play-date. My mind skipped and jumped until the man shifted and the bed creaked, bringing me back to the room. I took a deep breath and forced myself to look at his face. To really study it: his ruddy cheeks, the dark widow's peak at his hairline, his full lips.

He was once a baby, somebody's child.

I knew that hearing was the last sense to go before we die, and I began to hum "Amazing Grace," which was the first thing that came to mind. We were encouraged to hold patients' hands to create a warm physical connection, but I was too scared to touch him. I hummed the song over and over until his "death rattle," a crackling sound that occurs when a dying person is no longer able to swallow or cough, signaled that the end was near.

How sad to die like this, alone and chained to a bed.

After he stopped breathing, I sat for several minutes in silence, trying to process the intimate experience I'd just shared with a stranger, before pressing the call button to summon a nurse. I never even knew the man's name.

It took a few months before I was able to be fully present with the dying. In the early days, I felt I needed to make conversation, but in time I learned that it was often enough to just be there, even in silence.

Most of the hospice patients were elderly and could no longer communicate. I'd turn their hands over in mine, gazing at their age spots, wrinkles, and scars, and wonder what they'd done with those hands over their lifetimes. What had they created and touched before fate arranged our meeting in a cramped, sterile room? I wondered why they were alone and if they were afraid of dying.

Two decades later, the lessons I learned sitting with those who were dying would help me sit peacefully with my father and rest my hand on his forehead as he passed away. It would also help me prepare for my own death.

It was during my time as a hospice volunteer that I met the woman who would become my best friend and who would later stand by me when I made the decision to end my life. We met at a back-to-school night, just after Izzy started kindergarten. I sometimes struggled to make connections with other moms beyond talking about our children, but conversations with Susanne flowed easily right from the beginning. She had dark brown hair, a wide smile, and just a hint of a German accent. Her two daughters were in the same grades as mine.

Susanne had a knack for making the ordinary stuff of life funny and interesting. She was both refreshingly direct and openhearted. Her warmth was like falling into a hug, and she softened some of the sharper edges of my personality with her humor and gentle spirit. We began to meet up at local parks and, while the girls played, got to know each other better. If I was upset, I didn't need to put on a show for her, and the same was true for her. We could be real together. I confided in her about my MS diagnosis, and she told me that her partner, the father of her girls, was leaving.

I grew up believing in the fairy tale of romance. I've been fortunate enough to experience it, in all its glory—the euphoria, the obsession, and the deep abiding love. But over the course of my life, I've found what sustains me are my close female friends. Susanne was the one who would tell me if I was overreacting to an offhanded remark or gently suggest that ultra-low-rise jeans might not be the best look for me. She was the one who left flowers on my doorstep if I was blue or a pot of soup if I was ill. She became my person.

Her younger daughter turned to her at breakfast one morning and asked, "Why don't you just marry Diana?" We laughed and lamented, more than once, that we weren't lesbians.

One day as we rushed our kids through the school's entrance with a mob of other harried parents, I grabbed her arm. "Let's go to Burning Man!" I shouted over the din.

For years, I'd fantasized about attending the free-wheeling festival in the Nevada desert, an annual celebration of community, art, and self-expression. She laughed, assuming I was joking.

"I'm serious!" I yelled, as we pulled our children toward their classrooms. Her younger daughter dragged her feet and whined that she had a tummy ache. Susanne sighed, kissed the top of her head, and gave her a nudge through the door.

As we walked back down the hallway, she turned to me and winked. "I'm in!"

We set out to find outrageous outfits for an outrageous festival. At a shop on Haight Street, in San Francisco, I grabbed a black rubber catsuit and a Dolly Parton wig. Susanne bought a pink sequined cowboy hat and a sparkly sarong.

After making plans for the kids for the time we'd be gone, we loaded my minivan with camping gear and the second-hand bikes we'd glammed out with glitter. We drove seven hours northeast, over the Sierra Nevada mountains, to Nevada's Black Rock Desert.

The barren, dried lake bed, nicknamed "the playa," had been transformed into an otherworldly *Mad Max* landscape of giant, surreal, interactive large-scale art installations. Some thirty thousand people meandered about or biked around in eye-catching costumes, including, we counted, a group of about twenty-five Santas. Others sauntered about naked. Whenever the wind kicked up, the playa dust clouds swirled into the air, creating a gauze-like effect. People appeared and disappeared like mirages, and sediment coated everyone's skin with a fine gray powder, turning them into living ghosts.

Susanne and I reveled in the weirdness, dancing in blinding dust storms, engaging with provocative and soulful art, and striking up conversations with strangers. The festival operated on a barter economy, and I'd brought bundles of dried sage I'd picked from a trail near my house. I passed them out as I pedaled around the playa in my rubber catsuit, feeling light-years from my everyday life as a middle-aged mom. Burning Man's radical self-expression opened my senses in the same way that foreign travel did—and all without ever leaving the country.

At the end of the festival's nine days, each of the intricately built structures would be dismantled and the desert returned to a blank slate. It was that ephemerality of Burning Man that made it all the more magical.

I drove back home to Mill Valley with playa dust behind my ears and in my armpits, feeling awake and alive. Susanne and I promised each other we'd return every year until we turned ninety.

I never made it back.

2006 – 2007

After injecting myself with Copaxone three times a week for several years, I was alarmed to read that using it long-term could lead to hepatitis and even liver failure. My annual MRIs showed no further demyelination, so I asked Dr. Singh about stopping the treatment, and he hesitantly agreed. "Those are uncommon risks," he said, "but since your MS isn't proceeding in a typical fashion, we can take a break from Copaxone. You can always start again if you begin to get worse."

Over the years that I'd struggled with health issues, Bob did his best to shield me from stressors. The firm he'd started in his studio apartment closet had experienced the same meteoric rise as many of the dot-com companies he'd worked with. It also experienced the same setbacks. When the dot-com bubble burst, Bob lost many clients but assured me we'd be fine. He handled our finances while I focused on managing the kids and my health, which worked just fine for us—until it didn't. Bob came clean with me in the summer of 2006: We were broke. He emerged from his home office sheepishly holding a bowl of credit cards that he'd maxed out to keep us afloat.

"I'm so sorry," he said as we cut them into pieces and tossed them into the garbage. "I didn't want you to worry, and I always assumed that the market would bounce back."

Although I was upset with him, I was just as upset with myself. Even though I wasn't bringing home a paycheck, I should have been an equal partner in decisions that affected our finances. We agreed, from that point on, to create a budget and track expenses together.

But for the moment, we were in deep financial trouble. The only solution was to sell our beloved house, which we did, for a tidy profit. After we paid off our debts, there was enough money left over to put a down payment on a more modest home. We went to a few open houses but were disheartened by the crowds of would-be buyers scrambling to bid on a home in a tight real estate market. It was as if we were trapped on a hamster wheel, mindlessly going through the motions of chasing homeownership because that's just what we were expected to do as American adults.

In high school, I'd read Sinclair Lewis's satirical novel *Babbitt,* whose protagonist longs for passion and adventure and is thrown into crisis by the soul-deadening conformity of his middle-class life. Although the novel was published in 1922, it deeply resonated with me as a tenth grader in the 1970s, and now, as a middle-aged mother, I worried that I'd become a Babbitt myself.

As much as I loved being a mom, there were times when parenting was relentlessly tedious and mind-numbing. In my twenties and thirties, I'd backpacked through Zimbabwe and picked grapefruit on a kibbutz in Israel. My mantra was a Paul Coelho quote: "If you think adventure is dangerous, try routine; it is lethal." Now my life was regimented by routines: school, grocery store trips, and oil changes.

Shortly after we were forced to sell our home, my friend Elsbeth returned to the Bay Area after spending two years in New Zealand with her husband and two children. I wondered if we could do something similar. Maybe we could turn a setback on its head and do something extraordinary.

I raised the idea with Bob of taking a year-long trip. We'd long discussed visiting Nanchang, where Nunu had spent the first year of her life. After the adoption, we'd stayed in contact with her foster family, sending regular updates and photos as she grew.

After reviewing our finances, we determined we could pull it off if we lived on a shoestring budget. It was possible to travel extremely frugally in Asia; in many places, you could feed a family of four a meal for five dollars and rent a room for eighteen dollars a night. Oh, how I loved a bargain.

The idea took hold and blossomed. Bob's partner agreed to manage the day-to-day operation of their company while Bob continued to draw a minimal salary. I collaborated with the girls' teachers on kindergarten and second grade curriculums, purchasing workbooks and audiobooks.

We studied guidebooks and maps to piece together a seven-country itinerary that started in China and ended in New Zealand. We wanted to travel lightly and slowly, seeking authentic experiences over tourist traps. Since we couldn't speak the local languages in Asia, we hoped to forge connections by volunteering, exploring places off the beaten path, and spending enough time in each country to gain at least a basic understanding of its rituals and customs.

As we finessed the details, I got excited in a way I hadn't been in years. Travel was the opposite of routine. The opposite of being a Babbitt. I'd assumed that children would limit my ability to travel, but I began to see that they could be part of the adventure.

My ticking MS time bomb added urgency to the trip. Although the disease appeared to be in remission, Dr. Singh had warned me that this could change at any time, given the unpredictable nature of multiple sclerosis. Like a hibernating bear, there was no telling when it would roar to life and once again wreak havoc on my body. I was very aware of the possibility that I might only have a few good years left before it would become impossible to travel, and although we never directly discussed it, I knew Bob shared my concern.

The night before the new owners moved into our home, we spread our sleeping bags across the floor of the empty living room and lined up our travel gear by the front door—two rolling duffel bags, four backpacks, and four pairs of shoes.

I barely slept as I ran through my checklist. Did I pack the emergency antibiotics? *Yes.* Water filters? *Check.* Ziplock bags? *Yes.* At 5 a.m., as I tried to wake my daughters and hustle them out to the taxi, Susanne surprised us by arriving for goodbye hugs. Clasping my face in her hands, she said, "I want to be the last friend you see before you leave and the first friend you see when you get back."

A few hours later, I was buckled into a window seat of a 747, listening to the sound that never failed to bring me joy: the thrum of jet engines revving up. As was our custom, our family held hands across the aisle as the plane taxied down the runway and rose into the sky.

In Nanchang, we were welcomed with celebratory firecrackers by Nunu's foster family, and dozens of their neighbors poured into the street to greet us. Nunu was just thirteen months old when she left their care three years earlier. Now, at four, she was uncomfortable being the focus of attention, so Bob picked her up as we followed the family up six flights of stairs to their small apartment, where they offered us clay pot soup and slices of dragon fruit.

Much to everyone's delight, Nunu made herself right at home, pulling up a small chair and covering herself with a blanket. Photos were taken, relatives arrived, and gifts were exchanged. But Nunu had no interest in interacting with her foster parents, whom she no longer remembered. They kept trying to pick her up, but she refused their embraces. It was painful to see, but, eventually, with the help of a chocolate bribe, Nunu warmed to her first family. She even let Baba, her foster father, hold her as we walked down the street, later falling asleep on his shoulder. We spent several days with the family, relying on pantomime to communicate as we shared meals and went bowling.

After five days in China, we flew to Tibet, oohing at the cloud-ringed summit of Mt. Everest through the airplane windows. In Lhasa, we toured the seventeenth-century Potala Palace, where the Dalai Lama resided until 1959. A few days later, we settled into a shaded corner of the Jokhang Temple to watch a procession of Buddhist pilgrims spinning prayer wheels and chanting. After being troopers for several days, Izzy and Nunu were now restless and cranky. Nunu whined and asked if we could eat in a place that had a roof for once, so we ducked into a nearby restaurant for a meal of Tibetan dumplings and creamy yak butter tea. They continued to complain after we returned to the square, so I rummaged through my backpack and pulled out a craft project to keep them busy.

I'd packed yarn and beads to make simple necklaces, thinking it would be a fun way for the girls to connect with other people. We offered them to the Buddhist pilgrims, who looped them over their heads and pressed their hands together in a thankful gesture.

While Nunu had been a rock star in Nanchang, it was now Isobel's turn. We found ourselves surrounded by curious Tibetans who were visiting from remote villages and were mesmerized by our blonde, blue-eyed daughter. They wanted to touch her hair. They then gestured to Nunu and chatted among themselves, seemingly perplexed by how two Caucasians had created an Asian child.

After a week in Tibet, we traveled south to Vietnam for eight weeks, where we volunteered at local nonprofits, which we chose because they knew best what was needed in their own communities. We taught English at an elementary school and worked with HeartBeat Vietnam, an organization that provides free surgeries to children born with congenital heart defects. Before leaving California, we'd raised enough money to fund six operations. We traveled with the group's coordinator to rural villages to meet the children scheduled for surgery and process the required paperwork.

It was chilling to see children so ill—their defective hearts couldn't supply enough oxygen to their little bodies, giving their skin a gray pall. As we waved goodbye, I couldn't shake off a lingering unease. Most rural villages in Vietnam had no electricity, phones, or cars, and many residents couldn't afford bus fare to reach a hospital in Saigon. Was it just luck of the cosmic draw that we had easy access to healthcare? That we had the privilege of driving to the nearest emergency room or simply dialing 911?

After three months, we were road weary. When we reached Luang Prabang, Laos, it seemed like the perfect place to settle down for a while. An ancient village at the confluence of the Nam Khan and Mekong Rivers, Luang Prabang is known for its thirty-three gilded *wats,* or Buddhist temples. We found a simple unfurnished house for rent in the historic district, and after we were approved by the village chief, we paid the landlord in advance for a two-month lease, exchanging a thousand dollars for a six-inch stack of Lao kip.

Key in hand, we hailed a *tuk-tuk*, a three-wheeled scooter taxi, to the bustling Phousi market, where vendors sold everything from papayas to water buffalo meat to SIM cards. We bought six thin mattresses, four to sleep on and two to use as couches, and household supplies. When we moved into the house, the kitchen only had a sink. Several weeks later, the landlord delivered a stove and refrigerator, which were considered luxury items; many Lao families cooked over an open fire in front of their homes.

After tucking ourselves into our sleeping bags on the first night, we were jolted awake at 4 a.m. by a cacophony of drums, cymbals, and gongs coming from the *wat* across the street. The noise was so loud that the walls vibrated. We learned that the lunar calendar plays an important role in Buddhism and Lao culture and that the monks honored the phases of the moon. On every full moon, the monks shaved their heads to symbolize the practice of non-attachment and impermanence, one of Buddhism's main tenets.

The simplicity of life in Luang Prabang suited me. The girls wore clothes until they were visibly dirty, and I rotated between two skirts and gave up wearing underwear entirely. To make candle holders, we cut up plastic bottles and filled them with river sand. The girls decorated the bare walls with crayon drawings.

Our lives were slow, shorn of the frantic overscheduling that seemed to constitute life back home. We wandered the ancient city, visiting temples and markets. Or we stayed home, reading or making art.

Every morning, we followed the lead of our neighbors, who folded back the large wooden front doors of their homes that opened to the street to let in light and air. Chickens often wandered into our living room, much to the delight of the girls, who'd giggle and shoo them back out.

For dinner, we frequently visited the night market, where vendors tended pots simmering over wood fires or crouched on low stools as they split sugarcane with machetes. For a grand total of $2.50, our family of four ate a tasty meal of noodles chock-full of fresh vegetables as we sat at a long communal table. After dinner, we wandered among stalls filled with handmade crafts and textiles made by women from hill tribes in the north.

Nunu continued to draw stares and questions: "*Con Lao?*" (Is she Laotian?) "*No, no con Lao*," I'd respond. I'd point to both of my daughters and then to Bob and me, trying to communicate that we were parents of both girls while they patted her face in confusion.

Each morning at 5:30 a.m., a stream of barefoot monks in bright orange robes silently filed out of the wat across the way and walked down the street to collect alms of sticky rice and other food. The tradition of sharing, dating back seven hundred years, had strict customs and was beautiful to witness.

One afternoon, as Bob and I were making lunch, Isobel called from the living room, where she and Nunu were playing Go Fish on the tile floor.

"Mom! There's a monk at the door!"

Sure enough, a smiling, orange-robed novice stood in the doorway. He looked to be about eleven, a mere child himself. Laos has a long tradition of boys leaving impoverished rural areas to join Buddhist monasteries, offering them a way to get a decent education and regular meals. The novices follow a regimented schedule of chores, prayer, and study.

I had dipped my toe into the Buddhism waters during my first few years in San Francisco. I remembered the stillness I had felt after meditating on my living room rug, but I didn't recall ever being as peaceful as the people I met in Laos. Maybe it was their practice of nonviolence and compassion that gave them that presence. Maybe it was their belief in karma. Or maybe it was their relationships with spirits and ancestors.

I beckoned the boy inside, and he kneeled on the floor in front of the cards, eager to participate. The rules were obvious, so the language barrier wasn't an issue. His name, he told us, pointing at his chest, was Seng.

Back in the kitchen, Bob and I returned to dicing vegetables for soup. Squeals of laughter came from the living room, and we exchanged joyful looks. A few winters before, I'd been struggling with fatigue and pounding headaches. Now I was on the other side of the world symptom-free, listening to our daughters play with a young monk. I didn't know what the future held, or if I would get sick again, but in that moment, I was grateful for my renewed health.

The next day Seng returned with a friend. Our house soon became a magnet for young monks who popped over during study breaks. Their influence on our daughters was evident as Nunu and Isobel incorporated temple rituals into their play, pretending to be novices themselves—praying, chanting, creating altars, and collecting alms from Bob and me.

Several times a week, I volunteered at a local school, teaching monks English with the help of picture books. The sound "th" doesn't exist in the Lao language, and as I stuck my tongue between my front teeth to demonstrate how to pronounce the word "there," the monks burst into fits of giggles.

While I was teaching, Nunu was learning to read. One night at dinner, she pointed to a can of beer on the table and read out loud for the first time, carefully sounding out the brand name: "Beer Lao."

In January, Bob returned to California for six weeks to work on a big contract. We needed the money, so back he went. One morning shortly after he left, I woke feeling unusually fatigued.

Oh, shit. It's the "something's wrong" tired again.

As I dragged myself out of my sleeping bag to prepare breakfast, I felt as if I were wading through mud.

Is this MS? Should I have stayed on Copaxone?

I fed the girls and crawled back into bed. The full-body lassitude was followed by the same flu-like symptoms that had plagued me following a sinus infection a few years earlier—headaches, chills, night sweats, and nausea. When I Skyped with Bob, he offered to return to Laos, but I told him no. I knew he'd lose the contract if he did.

The last time I'd gotten sick, things had resolved on their own, so I hoped that would happen again. I wasn't overly concerned; I figured I just had to gut it out. I rose from bed only to cook, assign craft projects, or intervene in sisterly squabbles. During this time, I was especially grateful for the young monks who kept the girls occupied and brought cheer to the house.

After three weeks, I began to feel better, and within a few days of getting back on my feet, I announced to the girls that we were going on an adventure. We strapped on our backpacks, which we'd filled with water and snacks, and walked to the Mekong River, where we boarded a flat-bottomed boat and crossed to the opposite, less-inhabited, shore. We wandered down a dirt path and came across a small village of ten homes made of bamboo and palm and perched on stilts. A group of children playing tag stopped to look at us, and a voice called out, "Hello!" A young man with a broad smile approached and introduced himself as Leaun. He offered to show us around.

We walked past three women squatting on the ground, sifting rice through flat woven baskets. One paused to spit a stream of red betel nut juice into the dirt. Leaun, who'd studied English in school and spoke it well, asked if I'd like to try betel nut, a stimulant widely used throughout Asia.

Chewing betel nut with friends is akin to the Western custom of bonding over cocktails. Leaun spoke to the woman in Lao, and she offered me a big grin, her teeth stained maroon from years of chewing betel nut. She pulled a slice of dried areca nut from a small bag and slathered it with a white paste of slaked lime, which hastens the stimulant's absorption. She then tucked it into a betel leaf, along with a pinch of dried tobacco, rolling the concoction into what looked like a mini burrito.

My daughters watched wide-eyed as I slipped it between my lips. It was incredibly bitter, and I fought an immediate urge to spit it out. The women nudged each other and laughed as I grimaced, forcing myself to chew. I opened my mouth to show the girls my red teeth.

"Ewww!" they squealed. "You look like a vampire!"

Feeling a bit queasy, I spit the bundle onto the ground and thanked the women with a bow.

Leaun showed us his house, one of the few buildings in the village with a concrete foundation and a second floor. A window on the first floor opened to a small shop from which his family sold *Lao-Lao,* rice whisky, which they made in buckets and sold in recycled water bottles. In front of the house, Leaun's mother was dismembering a dead pig with a machete as his teenage sister squatted next to a tree stump, chopping the meat into small pieces. Nearby, his grandmother sauteed the minced pork with chilis, onion, cilantro, and noodles over an open fire. The intoxicating aroma of roasting meat was irresistible.

"Mama, I'm hungry," Isobel complained. We'd lost track of time, and it was now late afternoon.

Leaun invited us to join them for dinner—an unsurprising turn of events, given how welcoming Lao culture is—and we eagerly accepted. We sat on a floor mat around the communal platter, eating with chopsticks. Leaun refused my clumsy offer to pay, so I pulled out several pieces of the beef jerky I'd packed and offered them to our new friends. Leaun's grandmother snatched them from my hand and tucked them inside her blouse as everyone laughed.

By the time dinner was over, it was dusk. Leaun invited us to spend the night, telling us proudly that their house was the only one in the village with electricity. I glanced at my daughters, who both nodded excitedly.

To hell with toothbrushes and pajamas.

We followed Leaun upstairs to a small room lit by a single light bulb dangling from the ceiling. Two cozy mattresses covered with mosquito nets lay on the floor. We fell asleep to the backdrop of crickets and frogs and the occasional time-challenged rooster.

The next morning, we joined the family for a breakfast of fried rice and eggs, washed down with dark coffee sweetened with condensed milk. A girl about Isobel's age ran barefoot past the open doors of the house, craning her head to peek at us. After circling back, she lingered in the doorway, and we noticed a dirty rag tied around her foot as a bandage. That's when we realized none of the children wore shoes.

Leaun told us that the girl's father had died, and her mother was struggling to support her and her three younger siblings. I watched Isobel's eyebrows furrow with concern as he spoke. After he finished, she took off her beloved white and mint green sneakers, which she'd carefully picked out at the Bangkok airport to replace the worn-out pair she'd brought from California, and handed them to the girl.

"You can have them," she said shyly.

Leaun crouched down to translate. The girl sat on the ground to try them on. After Isobel showed her how to tie the laces, the girl shot to her feet and jumped up and down, testing the bounce of the rubber soles. "*Khob chai!*" she said with a wide smile. "Thank you." She pressed her hands together and held them to her lips; Izzy returned the gesture.

As the girl skipped away in Izzy's shoes, I watched an array of emotions flicker across my daughter's face. A little regret, perhaps, but also the warm pleasure that comes from giving without expecting anything in return, of doing something to ease another person's struggle. Izzy walked the mile back to the river barefoot, deep in thought as she held Nunu's hand.

There were rough patches during our stay in Asia, of course. The girls often balked at being dragged to yet another temple and complained during long, hot bus rides. "I'm bored to the bone!" Isobel once wailed, before announcing she was going to run away.

There were also political situations that made us uneasy. We cut short a visit to a friend in Nepal due to an uptick in hostilities between the government and communist insurgents, realizing it wasn't a good idea to drag two little kids into a potential war zone. I'd also hoped to visit Myanmar without worry, but once we arrived, we saw an overwhelming military presence and guarded civilians. Despite our desire to see more of the country, we knew soon after arriving that it was time for us to move on.

Health problems were an issue as well. We flew into Lhasa, which sits at twelve thousand feet, from Nanchang, which is at sea level, and a few hours later were overcome by altitude sickness. Cooped up in a spartan hotel room, sharing a single squat toilet in a tiny bathroom that lacked toilet paper, we were laid low by headaches, vomiting, and diarrhea. I tried my best to comfort the girls while feeling ill myself, but worried that my need for adventure had put my family's health at risk. We subsisted on water and airplane crackers for three days until we were well enough to continue our journey.

There were a few other scares. Bob got a severe case of conjunctivitis, which left him with red, weeping eyes; Izzy had a high fever, which we briefly feared was malaria; I twisted my ankle and hobbled around for a few weeks; and we all had periodic bouts of digestive distress. All these mishaps were par for the course during a year-long journey, but I often worried that a minor ailment would become something serious.

Traveling through countries where people had so few possessions was eye-opening for the girls. "Are we rich?" Nunu asked one day as we watched barefoot children in Myanmar kick a ball made of wadded plastic bags wrapped with string. I took a moment to compose my thoughts.

"There are many ways to be rich," I finally answered. "We may have more things than the people here, and life in California can be easier. But think about Leuan—he lives with his grandparents, they eat with their cousins, and they all take care of each other. Leaun is rich like that."

The girls nodded, and I was proud to have imparted an important life lesson. A few days later, however, when she was hungry and we couldn't find a restaurant, Nunu whined, "I want to go home. I want the easy life!" Bob and I burst out laughing.

In Cambodia, we visited the mystical twelfth-century temple, Ta Prohm, where the roots of the banyan trees had intertwined with the crumbling walls, as if the forest were swallowing it whole. Afterward, I wrote in my journal, "Its beauty lies in its union with nature—a reminder of the impermanence of life."

We went to a local carnival where we sipped sugarcane juice and ate lotus seeds, which tasted like slightly bitter hazelnuts. Aside from being a delicious snack, the lotus flower is sacred in Cambodia, symbolizing beauty, prosperity, and harmony. We were too afraid to try the durian fruit, whose smell, someone aptly noted, "was a mixture of turpentine and onions garnished with a gym sock." When we arrived at our hotel, we weren't a bit surprised to see signs banning the fruit, as well posters in English forbidding, humorously, "pets, fire, arms, explosives, inflammables, and stinking things."

In Bali, we spent a month in Ubud at a hotel on Monkey Forest

Road—aptly named given the way we had to shoo the animals from our breakfast table each morning. The monkeys were especially fond of hard-boiled eggs and snatched them from our plates if we weren't vigilant. We spent our days wandering around stone temples and watching dancers twirl to the beat of drums at festivals. In the coastal village of Pemuteran, the girls helped release newly hatched, endangered turtles into the sea.

We'd become a family of seasoned travelers. We'd learned to be flexible and to sleep in the same room—often in the same bed. We'd survived being sick, grouchy, and tired together. And we were creating enough memories to last a lifetime—jumping into the bathtub-warm emerald water of Vietnam's Ha Long Bay, watching the monks shave their heads on the full moon, and hiking through the jungles as monkeys swung overhead. We moved through the homeschooling curriculum with the girls as quickly as possible so we could get to the experiences that would truly teach them how to thrive—and be alive—in this world.

After nine months of bumping around Asia, we reached Nelson, New Zealand—a town perched on the Tasman Sea and bordered by national parks—where we enrolled the girls in a local school for three months. Although it was June, it was winter in the Southern Hemisphere, and the weather was cold, blustery, and rainy. We explored the South Island on the weekends, driving our rental car past herds of sheep that dotted the rolling green hills. It was beautiful, but it also felt isolated and empty. I missed the heat, the crowds, and the ebullience of Asia.

We settled into the familiar routines of school, regular meals, bedtimes, and bathing. But the return to a normal schedule conjured up a feeling of dread in me. I was nervous about going back to California, worried that the feeling of being fully alive would fade into the bland oblivion of the day-to-day.

It was in New Zealand that I once again started to feel more tired than usual, despite a clean, soft bed and plenty of sleep. I fueled myself with pots of black tea and took regular naps.

I wasn't ready to admit to myself that I might be getting sick again, and I didn't want to worry my family. After all, the symptoms would no doubt abate on their own, as they'd always done before.

2008 – 2010

We returned to Mill Valley after almost a year abroad. Shortly thereafter, we bought a three-bedroom, two-bath white clapboard home that reminded me of the beach houses on Cape Cod, where my family vacationed when I was a child. It was set in the foothills of Mt. Tamalpais, near Muir Woods and an abundance of hiking trails, and just a short drive from Stinson Beach.

There was a small backyard that was just big enough for a chicken coop. We'd all loved the curious chickens that wandered in and out of our house in Luang Prabang; keeping a few hens at our new home was a way to bring a bit of Laos home. We bought three downy chicks, which peeped in a box under a heat lamp in the living room until they were old enough to be moved outside.

After a year of living at a slower pace, returning to the States was like walking into a siren's blare; everything was frenetic and intense. The sheer number of products vying for attention at stores overwhelmed me, as did constant advertisements pushing everything from junk food to erectile dysfunction pills. After so much time in a different environment, this world struck me as overly loud and bright, and steeped in excess.

I missed life on the streets—the vibrant outdoor markets, the smiling vendors, the aroma of meat sizzling on open fires, the laughing children running barefoot and playing. Pushing a shopping cart down the neon-lit aisles of a grocery store left me numb. Everything was neatly packaged, impersonal, reduced. During a trip to Safeway, Isobel returned from picking out a box of cereal to find me crying in the produce section.

"I miss the markets in Laos," I said as she wrapped her arms around my waist.

"Missing a market is a funny thing to cry about." She repeated the advice I'd given her many times over the years when she was overwhelmed. "Breathe, Mama, just breathe."

The more I tried to cling to the magic of the trip, the more it slipped through my fingers and I found myself back on the hamster wheel of Western life. We'd had a car in New Zealand, but the roads were quieter there, and attempting to merge onto a busy California freeway made me curse like a sailor. The first time I filled the gas tank, I pulled away with the fuel hose still attached, the metal nozzle clattering down the road behind me.

After living in a culture where people cheerfully crowded onto buses and into *tuk-tuks*, I was struck by the number of solo drivers on the road. I was reminded of the opening scene of the 2004 movie *Crash*. "In any real city, you walk, you brush past people, and people bump into you. In LA, nobody touches you. We're always behind this metal and glass. I think we miss that touch so much, that we crash into each other just so we can feel something." Although I didn't live in Los Angeles, I felt an undercurrent of loneliness and missed touch as well—bus passengers squeezing past me with their bags of greens or gently shifting their hips against mine to make room for one more.

It had been eight years since my MS diagnosis and first MRI. Although I experienced bouts of fatigue, the tremors had mostly resolved, and my annual MRI showed that the white patches indicating demyelination of the nerve fibers in my brain hadn't expanded.

But that fall, out of the blue, I crashed. The "something's wrong" exhaustion returned, along with chills, night sweats, and headaches. I had to pry myself out of bed in the morning to help the girls get ready for school and slap together healthy lunches. The holidays were just around the corner, and I was dreading the flurry of activities and forced cheer they required.

I called Dr. Singh to book an appointment, wondering if I needed to start taking Copaxone again, but he didn't have an opening until January.

"What am I supposed to do until then?" I asked his receptionist, exasperated.

"I'm sorry, ma'am," she replied crisply. "That's the first opening."

The empathetic woman who'd slipped me in for an appointment was long gone; I had no choice but to muddle through until the new year.

One drizzly morning, I threw a jacket over my pajamas to drive the girls to school. *At least I'll look respectable through the car window.*

As I watched parents chatting with each other and hugging their kids, I grew jealous and angry. Once again, just as during my IVF days, I felt a creeping envy and deep desire to be part of what seemed an exclusive club: healthy parents enjoying a regular morning with their children and friends.

I wondered if exercising would help. In the past, post-workout endorphins had boosted my mood and energy levels. I signed up for a step class at the Mill Valley Community Center but felt winded just walking up the stairs to the gym. Nonetheless, I forced myself to follow the instructor's gyrations with the rest of the class.

Mind over matter.

After class, I felt a bit better and returned the next morning. This time, however, it was as though I were wearing a heavy rubber suit. The smallest movement was a struggle, and the instructor's peppy exhortations—*Come on! You got this!*—grated on my nerves. I left in the middle of class.

I slogged through the holidays, wrapping presents, baking cookies, and decorating the tree with a Christmas smile pasted on my face. But I had to spend more time napping to recover from the nonstop activities.

At our next appointment, Dr. Singh said that fatigue, numbness, and brain fog were common with multiple sclerosis, but flu-like symptoms were not. He was as puzzled as I was, so I decided to look for answers on my own. I'd put myself through graduate school as a paid researcher, so wading through studies and compiling data were second nature to me, and the internet held a cornucopia of specialized medical journals and peer-reviewed papers.

My research led me to Dr. Audra Spencer, or "Dr. Audra," as she preferred. She was an integrative medical doctor, which meant her focus was on deciphering the root cause of an illness rather than merely treating its expression. She had a reputation as an excellent diagnostician. She was also a walking advertisement for perfect health. A lithe brunette with cascading curls, she had a dazzling white smile and was always fashionably dressed in tasteful neutrals. Dr. Audra had hung her shingle more than ten years ago, but she still looked like a college coed.

When we met in her airy, plant-filled San Francisco office, she quizzed me about my symptoms before warmly reassuring me that we'd get to the bottom of my health crisis. She ordered a broad array of blood tests. Two weeks later, as I was putting away groceries, she called with the results.

"Good news, Diana," she said excitedly. "You've tested positive for Lyme disease."

I was confused. "Wait, I tested negative for Lyme at the MS clinic."

"I'm not surprised," she said. "Diagnosing Lyme disease isn't easy. Some tests are more sensitive than others. The test I used is highly accurate, and it's showing a clear Lyme result."

How could this be good news?

"Great, now I have Lyme *and* MS?"

"What?" She laughed. "No! You have Lyme, *not* MS. Lyme is often misdiagnosed as MS by doctors who are not Lyme specialists. Based on how long you've been sick, I believe you have what's known as Late-Stage Lyme Disease."

Hmmm. I needed some convincing.

"But I don't remember getting a tick bite. Or a rash. Aren't you supposed to get a rash?"

"Deer ticks are so small that many people don't even notice them," she said. "Some people—like you, apparently—don't feel the bite or get a rash. And here's why this is good news: Lyme can be treated."

I closed my eyes and let her words sink in. For almost a decade, I'd lived with fear and anxiety, waiting for the MS hammer to drop.

"What? Why didn't . . . ? " But Dr. Audra was in a hurry and cut me off.

"I have to run—I have a patient waiting—but let's get you in as soon as possible and start a treatment plan."

She transferred me to her receptionist, who booked an appointment for me later that week. I spent the rest of the afternoon on the phone, giddily calling family and friends to share the great news. "My medical mystery is finally solved!" "No blindness or paralysis in my future." "It's just Lyme." "It's treatable!"

Later that night, however, I lay awake and wondered, *If I hadn't made an appointment with Dr. Audra, how long would I have believed I had MS?*

When I canceled my next appointment with Dr. Singh, he called me back, concerned. I told him about the Lyme diagnosis and let him know that I was pursuing treatment with an integrative doctor.

"Well, just be aware there's a lot of controversy in the medical community about whether Late-Stage Lyme Disease is a true condition," he warned. I could tell from his tone that he was skeptical. "Your scans indicate that you may have MS, so it's important to keep track of it. Continue to come in for your annual MRIs, and let's see how it goes."

After we hung up, I googled Late-Stage Lyme, which confirmed what he'd said: The diagnosis was the subject of hot debate. The CDC does not recognize Late-Stage Lyme because of inadequate testing and scientific evidence, but there were many doctors who reported that their patients had symptoms long after the bacteria were cleared from the bloodstream. And then there were the conspiracy theorists who believed that the government had weaponized ticks to spread the disease.

I checked off the facts in my head: The MS wasn't progressing. My symptoms strongly suggested Lyme. And Dr. Audra was no slouch—she was, after all, a highly regarded chronic illness specialist and a graduate of Yale Medical School. I decided to continue working with her.

The first treatment consisted of two rounds of IV antibiotics to knock out any *Borrelia burgdorferi,* the bacteria that caused Lyme, that might still lurk in my body. I noted my daily symptoms in a journal and saw Dr. Audra twice a month. After three months, however, I wasn't any better.

"That just confirms my hunch," Dr. Audra told me at our next appointment. "Lyme can damage the immune system itself, so even though the bacteria are gone, your body is fooled into thinking they are still present and remains in attack mode. When your immune system activates, it releases chemicals that cause inflammation. That's why you feel like you have the flu all the time—your immune system is acting as if you do."

She leaned back in her chair and flashed her trademark smile. Dr. Audra had the energy and enthusiasm I didn't—I needed someone in my life confident I would get better—but I often found her exuberance exhausting. But who was I to say one of her many treatments wouldn't be the magic cure?

"Ok, that makes sense," I said. "Now what?"

She recommended a series of IV ozone treatments to control the inflammation. I was too sick to make sense of her explanations about L-2, TNF alpha, IL-6, and interferon gamma, but the gist of it was that ozone would stabilize my immune system.

A few days later, I found myself reclining in her clinic's "IV Room" as a nurse attached an IV line to my arm and watched as my dark red blood flowed up the tube into the clear bag hooked to the top of the pole. She then injected a large syringeful of ozone gas into the bag, which turned the blood a bright, bubbly red before it was returned, drop by drop, to my body.

I did ten ozone treatments, two a week for five weeks. I'd have more energy for a few days, triggering a spark of hope, only to crash again.

"Hang in there," Dr. Audra told me. "I've got another idea. We'll get to the bottom of this yet!"

That other idea was a new protocol that involved yet another series of IV drips, twenty this time, at four hundred dollars a pop. "These will support your cell membranes and mitochondria," Dr. Audra assured me.

From my high school biology days, I recalled that cell membranes filtered out toxins before they entered the cell and that mitochondria provide energy. The IV drips contained phosphatidylcholine, leucovorin, glutathione, and B12—an infusion, according to Dr. Audra, that would "restore optimal cell function."

Three times a week, for six weeks, I reported to the IV Room. The nurse used hot packs to dilate my veins, making it easier to insert a needle. Sometimes this took several minutes and more than a few painful pokes. I then sat in a recliner for an hour, reading, dozing, or imagining the IV drip acting as a liquid bricklayer, filling and smoothing the holes in my cell membranes.

After eighteen months of seeing Dr. Audra, I began to feel better for longer periods of time. I wasn't sure which treatment had helped, if the effect was cumulative, or if my symptoms had once again gone away on their own. It didn't matter; I was thrilled to be feeling more normal. Dr. Audra put me on a maintenance plan that included twelve daily supplements, a monthly ozone IV drip, and hormone replacement therapy because, she said, Lyme disrupts the body's estrogen and progesterone balance.

Now that I had my energy back, I started to think about returning to work. Between staying at home with the kids, traveling, and struggling with my health, I'd been out of the job market for more than a decade. Now that the girls were in first and third grades and more independent, it seemed like a good time to dust off my résumé.

Based on my experience fundraising for the Environmental Defense Fund, I landed a job as the Director of Development for the Coral Reef Alliance's San Francisco office. I'd be leading the fundraising department, raising money for reef protection and restoration around the world.

The girls were excited and helped me transition from yoga pants to business attire, giving a thumbs-up or thumbs-down as I pulled blouses and skirts from the back of my closet and arranged them on the bed. Susanne and her daughters came over for a dance party to celebrate this new phase of my life, and we blasted ABBA's "Dancing Queen" over the living room speakers.

My arms were marked with bruises from the never-ending needle pokes, but I was grateful to feel like a new woman—healthy, vibrant, and excited to be part of the world again.

2011 – 2017

How I relished the ritual of getting ready for work again! Applying a glossy lipstick, tucking my daily planner into my leather tote, and striding out the door, coffee cup in hand, to join the ranks of other career women. Bob dropped the girls off at school so I could take an early commuter bus, sipping my latte as we crossed the Golden Gate Bridge into San Francisco.

Each morning when I took in the view, I wanted to pinch myself. On clear days, the sun glinted off the bay, lighting the windows of the financial district in a golden glow. I had readjusted to Western life and felt blessed to live in such a beautiful part of the world.

The Coral Reef Alliance's office was on Market Street, in the heart of the financial district, next to a See's Candies shop. The sidewalks teemed with tech workers and tourists, bankers and street musicians. My colleagues were as passionate about protecting the environment as I was, and many traveled extensively to scuba dive. Sometimes I'd stay in the city for dinner, and we'd swap adventure stories in hip, buzzy restaurants. Depositing a paycheck into our bank account gave me a bump of confidence. I was back in the game.

I still had bouts of intense exhaustion, but I pushed through them and focused on my deadlines. I tossed back supplements, went for monthly IV treatments, ate healthy organic meals, exercised as much as possible, and shooed away negative thoughts.

I'm done being sick and I'm not looking back.

For two years, the universe granted me a reprieve. Then, despite being vaccinated, I got the flu. It should have been just that—the flu. But it wasn't. I stayed home, nursing a fever. After three days, it receded, and I returned to the office. But two weeks later, all the old symptoms roared back—headaches, chills, night sweats, and overwhelming exhaustion. Brain fog made focusing impossible. I couldn't write reports or run meetings, and I kept missing deadlines. I knew I was letting my colleagues down; instead of running the department, I was increasingly relying on my staff to do my job for me. My boss kindly suggested I cut back my hours for a month while I recovered, but no matter how much I slept or pushed myself, I wasn't able to fulfill my obligations. I emailed my director to resign.

Once again, illness had yanked the rug out from under me. Over the years, I hadn't found any discernable pattern to my bouts of sickness. Sometimes a downward spiral came out of the blue; other times there was a triggering event, such as a sinus infection or flu that escalated into a full-body assault. I did, however, notice one new and worrisome pattern: When I got sick, I was sick for longer. And when I did recover, it wasn't 100 percent. In my thirties, I usually bounced back after sleeping for twelve hours. In my fifties, that was no longer the case. Caffeine, in any form, no longer jump-started my brain, nor did the frequent pep talks I gave myself. As this pattern progressed, it was hard to focus on anything other than my crushing disappointment.

Baffled, I returned to Dr. Audra, who was still convinced that I had Late-Stage Lyme Disease.

"Managing Lyme can be very tricky," she said. "The bacteria can burrow into the tissues of the body." She suggested I repeat a round of IV antibiotics and another twenty IV treatments. She also wanted to change up my supplements.

Did any of this really *work the first time?*

I was dubious. After all, she hadn't cured me.

After mulling it over with Bob, I decided against following Dr. Audra's recommendations. I'd just quit my job and didn't want to spend thousands of dollars on out-of-pocket treatments that might not even help.

I wanted to find a doctor who had a different approach, one who would make me better for good. By this point, I'd become a regular on various internet forums where people discussed complex and chronic illnesses. One name kept popping up. Dr. Mossman was a holistic practitioner whose clinic was in nearby Sausalito, and he'd written a much-cited book on chronic illness. I phoned his office and booked the first appointment available, which was six weeks out.

Dr. Mossman was a rotund, older gentleman with a salt-and-pepper beard and professorial demeanor. His office was messy in an academic sort of way, with books piled willy-nilly on shelves and rows of documents stacked across his large mahogany desk. He reminded me of my father, who taught high school English and philosophy and whose home study was also lined with floor-to-ceiling bookshelves. That is to say, Dr. Mossman naturally inspired confidence.

After he reviewed the records I'd had sent over from Dr. Audra's office, Dr. Mossman ordered a host of new tests, including another one for Lyme, a stool analysis for parasites, blood panels to rule out exposure to viruses and heavy metals, and a urinalysis to check for mold exposure.

When I returned to his office to review the lab results, he had surprising news.

"The reports show several concerning factors," he said. "You've got significant levels of glyphosate and mercury in your blood. Glyphosate comes from eating pesticide-laden foods. The mercury is likely from your fillings."

"But that doesn't make sense!" I objected. "I only eat organic produce."

He lifted a hand to silence me, a gesture parents use to shush their kids. I tried not to feel offended.

"I'm just telling you what the report says. But here's what worries me most: You have very high levels of antibodies for the Epstein-Barr virus."

I stared at him in silence. *Epstein-Barr? What's next? Ebola?*

I knew Epstein-Barr (EBV) as mononucleosis, commonly known as the "kissing disease" because it spreads through saliva. Getting mono was almost a rite of passage in college, although I had no recollection of ever having had it.

"Most people are infected with EBV at some point in their lives and don't know it," he said. "But since you've had Lyme disease, even though it's no longer active, your immune system is compromised. The concern is that Epstein-Barr can trigger chronic fatigue syndrome."

I closed my eyes and rubbed my forehead, my mind spinning. "Hold on a second," I said. "I was diagnosed with MS thirteen years ago, but then Dr. Audra said I had Lyme, not MS. Now you're saying my symptoms are from Epstein-Barr?"

"You definitely had Lyme," he said. "But that's not what's making you sick right now. The good news is that Epstein-Barr is treatable."

I've heard that before.

"Okay," I said wearily. "Let's give it a try."

Dr. Mossman prescribed an antiviral medication and ultraviolet blood irradiation therapy, which uses UV light to kill pathogens. "You should start to feel better after eight to ten weekly treatments."

Two more months of feeling like crap?

I didn't have a better option.

I went home and broke the news to my family over the dinner table. "I'm going to need your help to get through this," I told them. Bob agreed to rearrange his schedule so he could pick up the girls from school, and they promised to step up and do more household chores.

At Dr. Mossman's clinic a few days later, I winced as a nurse inserted an IV line into the crook of my elbow. I watched as my blood coursed through a small brown box, where it was irradiated with UV light, and then as it dripped back into my arm.

Almost in passing, Dr. Mossman mentioned that the lab reports indicated I also had low levels of mycotoxins—poisonous substances produced by mold. He wasn't particularly concerned but suggested I test my house, just in case.

I ordered petri dishes of agar solution, which would capture any mold spores in the air, and placed them around my home. Three days later, I packaged them up and mailed them to a lab for testing. I was relieved that the analysis found negligible levels of mold in my house. When I reported the findings to Dr. Mossman, he suggested I must have been exposed to toxic mold in a previous home or workplace.

"Don't worry about it," he said. "I'll give you some supplements that will clean the mycotoxins out of your body."

Eliminating mercury was another matter. Dr. Mossman sent me to a "biological dentist" to replace my metal fillings with composites. The dentist and his assistant acted as if I were a biohazard, donning respirators and covering my body with a large rubber sheet with a single hole, allowing access to my mouth. An air purifier hummed loudly next to us. After the novocaine kicked in, the dentist drilled out the metal fillings in chunks to avoid vaporizing the mercury, which would send toxic fumes into the air.

For the next four years, my symptoms waxed and waned. I'd return to Dr. Mossman whenever I crashed. He tried to eliminate pathogens by prescribing another course of antivirals and ultraviolet treatments and to reduce inflammation with twenty-five sessions of hyperbaric oxygen therapy (HBOT). The HBOT therapy required me to lie in a small submarine-like chamber for two hours, inhaling pure, pressurized oxygen.

Repeated blood tests indicated that the Epstein-Barr titers had gone down, which was great, but I was still not at 100 percent—more like 75 percent. It was scary to think that I might never bounce back all the way, but what could I do but continue treatments? I swallowed the supplements, irradiated my blood, and fell into bed at 8 p.m. each night, hoping I'd wake up in the morning with more vitality than I'd had the day before.

It was during an upswing a year later that a dream job drifted into my life like a golden feather. I was feeling just healthy enough to reach out and grab it. In Laos, I'd met a woman who led overseas tours for Stanford University's alumni association. "I want *your* job!" I'd told her.

We stayed in touch and five years later, she contacted me out of the blue to say they were looking to hire a new guide. It was very part-time, just three fourteen-day trips a year. I could certainly handle that. I drove an hour down to Palo Alto for the interview, dressed in my favorite sky-blue silk blouse and black tailored pants. A few days later, the director called me with happy news: I was going to be *paid* to travel. The morning after I was offered the job, I woke up to find a celebratory bouquet of daffodils and a family-sized bag of M&Ms on my doorstep, courtesy of dear Susanne.

In 2014, I led small groups of Stanford alumni on trips to Morocco, Japan, and the Baltic states, herding them onto private tour buses and into hotels, restaurants, and world heritage sites. After traveling on the cheap for most of my life, I was now basking in luxury, staying in five-star hotels and enjoying meals prepared by private chefs. The alums—mostly retirees—occasionally got cranky over dietary issues or bad weather, but for the most part, the job was perfect for me.

Now that I had more energy, I found myself feeling restless between trips. Before our year-long sojourn in Asia, I'd stopped working as a hospice volunteer and I considered returning to Marin General. I kept thinking of the San Quentin patient who'd died handcuffed to the bed. Each time I drove west on the Richmond-San Rafael Bridge, I became increasingly curious about the enormous prison complex, which jutted into the bay, and the thousands of men living behind its imposing walls.

One afternoon I googled "San Quentin volunteers." After reviewing a few options, I signed up for a program that prepared prisoners to reenter society by giving them leads on potential jobs and housing. Few opportunities were available to the newly released men, which was part of the reason two-thirds of them returned to prison. I figured I had enough energy to volunteer one night a week.

I wasn't sure what to expect. Entering the prison "yard"—a recreation area surrounded by four guard lookout towers and high granite walls topped with razor wire—was intimidating. As I watched a group of muscular inmates lifting weights, it was as though I'd walked onto a staged movie set.

Although many of the men had tough exteriors and prominent

gang tattoos, they were grateful for the program and exceedingly polite as they sat across a small table from me. But I soon understood that applying for jobs from "the inside" was nearly impossible. The program had compiled just a single sheet of job leads and inmates didn't have internet access, so they sent handwritten letters to potential employers. Not surprisingly, few responded; most employers are reluctant to hire a convicted felon sight unseen.

At a more basic level, most of the men didn't know how to prepare for an interview, craft a résumé, discuss their skill set, or talk about their criminal histories with a potential employer. Some had never held a legal job.

I created a new fourteen-week program, the Prison to Employment Connection, which was designed specifically to teach inmates job-readiness skills. The weekly class would culminate with a job fair at the prison.

The first time I stood before a room of prisoners as a teacher, I was so nervous that I sweated through my blouse. Over time, however, I grew more comfortable with them and they, in turn, learned to trust me. They realized I was there to support them, not judge them. While I never excused the behavior that landed them in prison—most of them deserved to be there—I also knew it was better for society at large if the men were able to return to their communities and find work. Their self-esteem and ability to adapt to life outside of prison depended on it.

Between classes, I cold-called local companies that offered entry-level positions, including restaurants, construction firms, and HVAC installers, and was thrilled to find that many of them were willing to take a chance on the formerly incarcerated. Over time, I established relationships with more than forty employers who visited San Quentin to interview our graduates face-to-face. The program was the first of its kind in any of California's thirty-five prisons.

I found it ironic that at age fifty-five, I'd found a deep sense of purpose—and in a prison, no less. I was inspired by the words of the indigenous Australian activist Lilla Watson, who wrote, "If you have come here to help me, you are wasting your time. But if you have come because your liberation is bound up with mine, then let us work together."

After a few months, however, I once again began to wake up with pounding headaches and feeling sapped of energy even after a good night of sleep. *Oh shit. How am I going to make it through the day?*

I'd gotten pretty darn good at gritting my teeth and going through the motions, but operating at 75 percent capacity soon became 50 percent, and then unable-to-get-out-of-bed percent. I sometimes had to cancel my San Quentin class.

In the spring of 2015, I was scheduled to lead a Stanford tour to the Galapagos Islands when I hit a particularly rough patch. I'd been counting down the days to the trip, showing my daughters photos of blue-footed boobies and five-hundred-pound tortoises—animals that weren't found anywhere else in the world—and fantasizing about swimming in isolated bays of turquoise water ringed with pristine white sand beaches.

I'd been able to push through previous trips by getting extra sleep and boosting my supplements, but now I was getting worse by the day. I called Dr. Mossman in a panic, and he suggested a supplement called "ATP Fuel" to jump-start my mitochondria and energy levels. I had it shipped overnight. But after ten days of taking five capsules before breakfast and five before lunch, I didn't notice the slightest improvement in my brain fog or exhaustion. It was with a heavy heart that I emailed my boss two weeks before the trip to let her know I was resigning. I was in no state to lead groups down uneven trails of lava rock.

She called me right away, gently inquiring about my malady. I told her I had Lyme disease and that it was getting harder to control. Over time, I'd found it easier to blame a known diagnosis than try to explain the details of a constantly shifting illness.

The first months after I quit my job passed in a blur of fatigue. One evening, I dragged myself to a friend's birthday party. I'd already turned down several invitations from her and knew that I needed to channel some of my limited energy toward my friends or I'd end up losing them.

At the party, I noticed another woman who also appeared to be struggling to socialize, and we found ourselves in the same corner of the living room. She kept sneaking glances at her watch, clearly as eager to leave as I was.

"Do you have any sense of when the cake will appear?" she asked with a pained look.

"I feel you," I said. "I'd like to get out of here too—I'm not feeling very well."

It turned out that she'd recently completed both chemotherapy and radiation for breast cancer, but her tumors had barely shrunk. "I've cut my hours way back at my law firm because I feel like hell all the time," she said.

But then her eyes lit up as she told me about the Viva Institute and its radical new therapy, called the "Viva Regimen." "It's my next option," she said. "It uses the body's own energy to heal itself. I've heard of several people who are now cancer-free after completing it."

Just talking about the treatment changed her demeanor. Well, if the Viva Regimen could cure cancer, it seemed possible that it could end the drumbeat of flu-like symptoms I'd been fighting on and off for the past two decades.

When I got home, I crawled into bed next to Bob and looked up the Viva Institute's website on my laptop. I was too tired to read the text, so I watched the videos instead. One featured the Viva Institute's founder, Dr. Crenshaw, a large man in his late forties with a serious, self-assured demeanor. He explained that the Viva Regimen addressed cellular dysfunctions that caused more than twenty chronic illnesses, ranging from cancer to Lyme to autism.

I rolled my eyes. *Of* course *it cures everything.*

But there were also multiple video endorsements from doctors not affiliated with his company, as well as glowing testimonials from grateful patients who said that "the Viva" had restored them to full health. A man with Lyme disease claimed he'd recovered enough energy to return to playing basketball several times a week. Cancer patients who said they'd received terminal diagnoses were teary-eyed as they described their new lease on life. It was hard not to feel emotional as I listened to their moving declarations. That night, as I snuggled into my down pillow and drifted off to sleep, I felt excited and hopeful for the first time in months.

The next morning, after calling the Viva Institute and speaking to a representative, I was increasingly optimistic about the treatment. It entailed a strict dietary and detox regimen, followed by a four-week stay at a clinic in the Bahamas, where patients underwent a series of treatments with patented machines that cleared their bodies of disease-causing microorganisms.

The biggest hiccup was the hefty price tag: $16,995.

Jesus.

I emailed Dr. Mossman to get his opinion. He wasn't familiar with the regimen, but he looked at the website and noticed that one of his colleagues had endorsed it. "We've worked on cases together and I respect her opinion," he wrote back.

I talked it over with Bob. He'd offered unwavering support over the years, but this was the most expensive treatment I'd pursued yet.

"If you think it might work, then go for it," he said. His business was booming again thanks to the rebounding tech industry. We ran the numbers and decided it was important enough to pull money out of our savings account.

I signed a contract with the company that instructed me to wire the funds to a bank in Switzerland. I was so excited that it didn't strike me as unusual that the company's entire operation—its banks and clinic—were offshore.

For the next six months, I followed the regimen that would prepare me for the more advanced therapy in the Bahamas. My daily schedule was so rigorous that I created an Excel spreadsheet just to keep track of the details. Upon waking each day, I peed on a strip of paper to test the pH levels of my urine, then logged the results on the patient portal, along with any symptoms I was experiencing.

The rest of the treatment revolved around a complicated protocol of juice cleanses, colonics, and swigs of diluted apple cider vinegar. I was instructed to only drink distilled water. There was a lengthy list of forbidden foods: alcohol, caffeine, all spices, white sugar, and flour, as well as entire sections of the produce department. Every day I dutifully swallowed a fistful of supplements and drank three cups of distilled water seasoned with drops of food-grade hydrogen peroxide intended to kill any remaining pathogens.

The patented sprays arrived in a small white metal case containing ten glass vials. The first time I spritzed the slightly sweet liquid under my tongue, I closed my eyes and imagined tiny luminous bubbles rushing through my system, scrubbing it free of germs and restoring my immune system.

At first, I had more good days than bad. *It's actually working!*

Then, for no apparent reason, I went downhill again and had to cancel a trip for my thirty-fifth college reunion. By late May, I was back in bed. I stuck with the daily treatments, but by mid-June I was so ill I worried I wouldn't be able to travel to the Bahamas for the final phase of the regimen.

A Viva representative told me that my intense symptoms were likely a good thing. Dead pathogens were piling up faster than my body could excrete them, he said, which was making me feel sick. In other words, the treatment was working. I'd heard that exact explanation before, from Dr. Audra and Dr. Mossman. It sort of made sense, so I didn't press the matter. After all, who was I to second guess doctors? I had invested so much time, energy, and money into this process—I couldn't imagine it wasn't working.

I flew to the Bahamas in early July of 2016. A representative from the clinic picked me up from the airport, and for the next two hours I watched the Bahamian flag hanging from his rearview mirror dance as we bounced over bumps and through potholes until we reached our destination. We drove past the "No Worry Grocery," a squat teal building, before arriving at the dated hotel that would be my home for the next month.

The hotel was within walking distance of the clinic, and early the next morning, I followed signs down a path that wound through dense jungle. When I rounded the final bend, I was surprised to discover that the clinic wasn't the modern, tile-clad building I'd imagined but a simple clapboard house.

Interesting. But hey, it's the Bahamas. They do things differently here.

When I walked through the door, the smiling staff ushered me to the dining room, where I joined two other patients eating a breakfast of spelt muffins and herbal tea. One had late-stage breast cancer and the other was battling Lyme. As we chatted, two American men walked in, Dr. Sebastian and Dr. Mower, who introduced themselves as "doctors of naturopathic medicine." They wore matching black t-shirts with the company name embroidered on the left side of the chest.

"We're so glad you're here, Diana," said the younger one, Dr. Sebastian. He leaned down and put a hand on my shoulder, gently squeezing it. "Don't worry, we're gonna get you all better."

I reached up and covered his hand with mine. "Thank you," I said, my eyes stinging.

After breakfast, I went upstairs to the treatment room, which was furnished with a recliner and a small table holding a water pitcher. A wheeled cart held a microwave-sized machine covered with dials and flashing lights. Dr. Sebastian told me this was the Z-7 Mitochondrial Disruptor, which "takes advantage of the role of energy generated within the mitochondria, to heal the cellular system." He handed me two metal bars that were wired to the machine and flipped a switch. The machine began to hum, and for the next few hours, I clutched the bars in my lap, dozing and watching the palm trees sway through the screened window as the frequencies thrummed through my body.

The concept behind the treatment made sense to me. After all, humans are made up of cells, which are made up of atoms, which themselves are just particles, and those particles are just vibrations. Even Albert Einstein thought so, famously stating that "everything in life is vibration."

I forced myself to think positive thoughts. *Healing. I'm healing.*

When the treatment ended, it was time for lunch—although I quickly learned not to get too excited about food breaks. All meals consisted of salt-free, gluten-free, vegetarian fare prepared by Dr. Crenshaw's twenty-something daughter. They were exceedingly healthy but also tasteless; I certainly wasn't running into the kitchen to devour the sugar-free, chickpea flour muffins as they emerged hot from the oven. Nonetheless, the food inspired confidence: If meals were so carefully planned and researched, I figured the treatments must be as well.

In the afternoon, I went back upstairs, where I underwent treatments with more machines that were supposedly coursing healing vibrations and energy throughout my body. Dr. Sebastian, spouting mind-numbing jargon, gave me lengthy explanations about what each machine did. I had no idea what he was talking about, so I just nodded and smiled politely.

Next came the Proton Frequency Radiator, whose plasma tube broadcasted more healing frequencies. To pass the time, I listened to music on my phone and dipped into the latest Jodi Picoult novel. I didn't feel immediate results from the machine therapies, but I was happy not to be languishing in California with my bedroom curtains drawn.

I will do whatever I have to do and eat whatever I have to eat to get better.

One morning during breakfast, Dr. Crenshaw joined us at the table. He was wearing a crisp white lab coat and exuded an aura of celebrity. Everyone fell silent and turned to face him, but he said little as he scarfed down a dry muffin.

"It was such a long trip to get here from California," I said in an attempt to draw him out. "I hope you open a clinic in the States soon!"

He plunked his coffee cup down and gave me a sour look. "That's not going to happen. We have to operate outside of the United States."

"But we're all Americans here," I continued more quietly, feeling a bit intimidated. "Why not?"

He laughed. "We're having so much success curing disease that Big Pharma has it in for us. When you disrupt Big Pharma's income stream, they don't like it. They're trying to suppress unconventional treatments like ours, which is why I've been receiving death threats."

"*Death* threats?" I asked.

"They're out to stop us any way they can," he replied.

He stood abruptly, ending the conversation. I watched him walk away, then caught the eye of the cancer patient. She shrugged before averting her eyes and taking a drink of her fresh pineapple juice.

During the four weeks I spent at the clinic, I heard one phrase repeatedly: Big Pharma. When I told Dr. Crenshaw about the antibiotics and antivirals I'd taken prior to starting the Viva Regimen, he muttered, "Those are garbage drugs, and they aren't getting to the root of the problem. Did you get any better after taking them? Think about it. Drug companies make money by keeping you sick."

Well, he has a point there.

I knew the pharmaceutical industry had a history of valuing profits over people. There'd been a recent spate of exposés in the mainstream press detailing how numerous companies had suppressed data on the harmful side effects of their drugs to get FDA approval. Some had even paid doctors kickbacks for prescribing their products.

I felt as though I'd joined an underground movement that would forever change the face of medicine. The treatment seemed to be working, and by the end of my stay, I had more energy and suffered from fewer flu-like symptoms. It was exciting to think that this cutting-edge protocol could help countless patients wean themselves from a dependency on evil drug manufacturers.

Or so I wanted to believe.

I flew home feeling rejuvenated. I hoped and prayed that my new-found energy would last. I continued chugging the diluted apple cider vinegar, spraying the patented solution under my tongue, and following a low-acid diet.

That fall, I was well enough to take Izzy on a tour of eight liberal arts colleges in New England. Strolling past elegant brick lecture halls and students sporting new backpacks, the nip of fall in the air, I recalled my own excitement as a college freshman. As we drove from tour to tour, we listened to Izzy's favorite band, The Chainsmokers, and she summarized her impressions of each campus. I was thrilled to be able to support her through the next big step in her life.

Three months after our college tour, however, I was dropped-kicked again: exhaustion, night sweats, recurring headaches, and nausea. It was as if I'd never done the Viva Regimen to begin with.

When I emailed Dr. Sebastian, he suggested I return to the Bahamas. "We just acquired a new oscillator that would be perfect for you," he said. "We could offer you a returning client discount, so it would cost you only $13,599."

He sounded like a used car salesman calling out after a potential buyer walking off the lot. I didn't even have the energy to get angry. "I'll have to think about it," I responded weakly before hanging up.

I felt both defeated and angry. Almost twenty thousand dollars down the drain. I'd later discover that the Viva Institute was a fraud. Although there were times I felt better during the treatment, I now chalk that up to the vagaries of my illness rather than the treatments.

A few years later, an FDA investigation revealed that Dr. Crenshaw had received a doctorate from a diploma mill in the Caribbean. And although he claimed that the Viva Regimen was backed by extensive clinical research, that was an outright lie. There were no published studies or clinical trials to be found, just a trail of hype, including flashy videos, paid endorsements, and performative "treatments."

I was devastated to learn that many of the patients whose glowing testimonials appeared on the website had died soon after completing the regimen. Reading interviews with their furious, grieving family members, I cried.

As I read page after page detailing the Viva scam, I wondered if Dr. Crenshaw and his associates had ever believed that their treatments worked, or if they had devised the entire program solely to profit from the desperately ill—exactly what they accused Big Pharma of doing.

The FDA revelations led to the closure of the clinic, but it's hard to stamp out snake oil peddlers. Dr. Crenshaw later resurrected the regimen, once again hawking a bogus product online as a miracle cure.

Six years later, Dr. Sebastian, one of Dr. Crenshaw's associates, contacted me out of the blue, trying to sell me on a new machine he'd built to "restore mitochondrial function." He was now treating patients in the States under his own shingle. When I pressed him about why the original clinic had gone under, he quickly changed the subject. Later, he admitted to working as an Uber driver in Atlantic City to make ends meet. I told him I wasn't interested and quickly ended the call.

In hindsight, all the signs were there: the slick marketing, the fast-talking pitchmen, the too-good-to-be-true results. But when you're chronically unwell, it's easy to ignore red flags. Desperation hooks us on hope. Each time I went downhill, it was hope that allowed me to power through my days and to mother my children—even to get out of bed. I had to believe that eventually, somehow, I would find a cure. It was the only way forward.

2018

Back to the drawing board I went, searching for an elusive cure. I scoured internet boards dedicated to chronic disease, and based on user recommendations, started working with two new doctors. The first treated me for a "faulty endocrine system." The second said that I had "a leaky gut," and suggested I consider a fecal transplant.

Increasingly desperate, I jumped from doctor to doctor. Each focused on a different issue, unable to put all the pieces together and unwilling to collaborate with the others.

I was also struggling with the disintegration of my twenty-year marriage. From the outside, Bob and I appeared to be the perfect couple, and in many ways we were. We had similar interests and values and shared a common parenting style.

But over the years, a distance had grown between us. It was as if we were separated by a plate glass window, unable to reach each other. I had a degree in psychology and was eager to talk through the petty resentments, misunderstandings, and other issues that accumulate in any long-term relationship. But to Bob, such marital tête-à-têtes were about as appealing as undergoing a root canal. We went to couples counseling, hoping an impartial mediator could help, but the more I pushed him into soul-searching discussions, the more he pulled away.

In truth, we had fundamentally different styles of connecting. Bob was an extrovert who thrived on being busy and diving into his work. He often traveled on business, and when he was home, he was usually on the go, heading into the city for dinner or to attend a show. Everybody, including me, loved his even-tempered and generous character. But I was an introvert who found chitchatting at social events to be tedious, preferring intimate talks and introspection. I needed a deep connection to feel grounded and loved.

While I certainly enjoyed the finer things in life, the truth of the matter was that we were just different: He was wine, I was beer. He was a luxury hotel, I was a hostel. He was steady, I was restless.

My ongoing health problems further complicated our relationship. In the worst of times, when I spent listless days in bed, I encouraged Bob to take the girls on our planned vacations and to socialize with his large circle of friends. I didn't want to drag him—and them—down. Yet on days when I was acutely unwell, our lack of a deep connection exacerbated my sense of loneliness.

We finally acknowledged—with both profound grief and the relief that comes with articulating the truth—that our relationship had run its course.

We held a ceremony to honor the end of our marriage in the same place we were wed. Elizabeth, who had married us, guided us through a dissolution ceremony. We read statements of gratitude to each other and slipped off our rings, eager to move on to the next phase of our relationship, which included focusing on co-parenting our two teenage daughters.

One winter night, Bob and I met at a coffee shop to finalize our divorce papers, and my life was further upended. I'd stepped outside to fetch a document from my car, and as I returned to the café, a car slammed into me in the middle of the crosswalk.

I don't remember being hit. Or flying through the air. Or bouncing off the car's hood and landing on the pavement. What I *do* remember was the screech of tires and the glare of headlights as I lay sprawled on my back in the street.

The driver who hit me, a young woman with blonde hair, kneeled beside me, her face hovering anxiously above mine. "Oh my God! I'm so sorry! I didn't see you!"

She helped me to my feet and supported me as I hobbled to the curb and sat down. A small group gathered around us, including a bearded man who told us that he'd called 911. I felt nauseated and began to shake, and an older woman draped her coat over my shoulders.

A teenager rode by on a bike, then circled back to look at the car. "Jeez! That's a big hole!"

I lifted my eyes and saw a melon-sized crater in the windshield of a blue Honda. It slowly dawned on me that the hole had been made by my head. A spiderweb of broken safety glass radiated from the opening.

An ambulance barreled toward us, siren blaring and lights flashing. It screeched to a halt, and two paramedics hopped out. One opened the back doors and yanked out a gurney. The other squatted in front of me. He bore an uncanny resemblance to the incredibly handsome actor Idris Elba, which somehow made everything even more surreal.

"Idris" gently probed my spine and head.

"Are you in pain?" he asked.

"Head," I croaked.

"Are you having trouble breathing?" I winced as I shook my head no.

The paramedics fitted me with a cervical collar, secured me to a spine board, and lifted me onto the gurney. Out of the corner of my eye, I saw a pair of police officers interviewing witnesses and the driver.

Bob wondered where I was, and after hearing the siren, came

to look for me. He saw me being loaded into the ambulance and followed it to the hospital, calling Susanne on the way and asking her to bring Nunu.

Inside the ambulance, Idris hooked me up to oxygen as we sped to the hospital. I felt calm and strangely removed from the situation, probably the result of a rush of pain-suppressing adrenaline. I remember looking up and admiring Idris's face, feeling that I was in good hands.

By the time Bob, Susanne, and Nunu tracked me down in the ER, they were astonished to find me yakking away on my cell phone. The adrenaline had given me a bad case of motormouth, and I was speed-dialing friends and family to let them know what had happened.

"I just survived getting hit by a car!" I exclaimed to a shocked friend. Susanne gently pried the phone from my hands.

X-rays showed no broken bones, and an MRI indicated there was no brain bleed. What I *did* have, however, was confusion, dizziness, and a horrific headache that was exacerbated by the hospital's buzzing fluorescent lights. A doctor gave me an anti-inflammatory and a potent cocktail of painkillers, which quickly knocked me out.

When I opened my eyes the next morning, the first thing I saw was Susanne's smile; she'd spent the night in the armchair next to my bed. Bob had taken Nunu home and phoned Izzy, who was a freshman at Wesleyan, to tell her I'd been in an accident. Susanne had insisted on staying with me.

"Morning, sleepyhead," she said, sweeping the hair off my forehead before ringing the call button for breakfast. When the tray of food arrived, I was dismayed to find that everything tasted the same: eggs, potatoes, bacon, even the orange slices. I had anosmia, an inability to smell, which is related to the sense of taste. The neurologist told me that anosmia was common with head injuries and usually temporary.

In my case, however, it wasn't. I still can't smell or taste much of anything. Even homemade chocolate chip cookies, one of my favorite treats, are about as flavorful as cardboard.

What I didn't yet know was that the loss of taste would be the first of many new losses to come.

A later MRI indicated that I suffered "bilateral anterior-inferior frontal lobe encephalomalacia." In other words, a softening or loss of brain tissue. In short, I had a traumatic brain injury (TBI). There was no specific treatment, and after five days I was discharged with strict instructions: Lie in a dark room with your eyes closed. Move as little as possible. No visitors. No electronic screens. No music. The idea was to allow my brain to heal by taxing it as little as possible.

For the first few weeks, I lay flat on my back, bored out of my mind. Bob and Susanne organized a meal train, but nobody was allowed to stay and visit. Nunu became my nurse, bringing me trays of food and making sure I stayed hydrated. When I couldn't stand looking at the bedroom walls any longer, I wobbled downstairs and sprawled out on the couch. Although I was no longer dizzy, I was spacey and unable to concentrate. I tried to meditate, visualizing my brain healing, but it was too hard to focus for more than a minute or so. Sometimes I defied the doctor's orders and replied to emails and texts.

Once I was cleared to move around, I went to physical therapy to address the pain of a severely bruised coccyx and to realign my neck, which had been wrenched in the crash. Several months of therapy resolved some of my physical discomfort, but the head injury left me with something far worse: a tidal wave of severe depression.

Although as many as three in five traumatic brain injury survivors experience depression, the rates for people with prior depressive episodes are even higher. The doctors at the hospital never mentioned it, but I later learned that head trauma can alter neurotransmitters, the prefrontal cortex, and the limbic system, all of which are involved in regulating emotions. Like the spiderweb of broken glass that radiated outward from the spot where my head hit the windshield, the effects of my TBI continued to reverberate long after the accident. Blindsided by a crushing sense of despair, my only relief was sleep. But as soon as the morning light struck my face, I fell back into a black hole of depression.

When spring came, my beloved garden lay fallow. I couldn't muster the energy to go outside and welcome the first daffodils of the season. I couldn't plant vegetables. I couldn't bend down to pull invasive weeds. Friends brought gifts and food, washed my dirty dishes, watered the wilting houseplants, and encouraged me to take my recovery one day at a time. Most days, however, I could only manage minute to minute.

One afternoon, I was resting on the sofa when the doorbell startled me awake. I dragged myself up to answer it and saw a friend—more an acquaintance, really—bearing a tall bouquet of sunflowers.

"I left you a voicemail a couple of weeks ago and you never got back to me," she said reproachfully.

I didn't have the bandwidth to manage her hurt feelings. I just wanted to give her a quick hug and send her on her way so I could flop back down on the couch.

"Please don't take it personally," I said. "I've been a little depressed lately."

She lingered, and I felt obligated to invite her in. As she entered my living room, she gestured grandly, sweeping her arm in a semicircle.

"How could you be sad living in this *beautiful* house?"

Sad? I would have given anything to merely feel sad. I wasn't experiencing the kind of passing bad mood caused by a fight with a boyfriend or a bad performance review. My brain had been profoundly, and I feared permanently, altered. But there were no bandages to show for it; I looked perfectly "normal."

I forced myself to chat for a few minutes before ushering her out. After she left, I slumped against the door, weeping—not just from physical or even emotional pain, but because it seemed nobody could understand the peculiar nature of my agony. Not for the first time, I wished I had a visible, bleeding wound that people could see, and that would elicit understanding and sympathy.

The woman was one of several well-meaning people who faded from my social circle during this time. Most just drifted away, unable to grasp what was wrong with me and not knowing how to help. I let them go.

Susanne, however, was always there for me, tailoring our activities according to my energy levels. Some days all I could handle was propping myself up on a bench in the town square, the same place where we had sat cross-legged on the ground while our young daughters played tag and hopscotch. Now we watched strangers walk by, occasionally entertaining ourselves by making up sordid stories about their private lives. Most of the time, however, I remained mired in darkness, often barely speaking. On my worst days, I was only able to respond to Susanne's texts with a single "." to let her know I was still alive.

This suffocating darkness was far worse than the postpartum depression I'd experienced after Izzy was born. At Susanne's urging, I began seeing a psychiatrist, Dr. Rosen, who put me on a revolving door of eight antidepressants to treat what he diagnosed as major depression. I tried different doses and combinations of medications including Wellbutrin, Prozac, and Celexa. Some made me so sleepy I'd nod off mid-sentence. Others made me dizzy. None made a dent in the wretched bleakness that dogged me around the clock.

The British journalist Sally Brampton perfectly captured the feeling of depression when she described it as a landscape that "is cold and black and empty. It is more terrifying and more horrible than anywhere I have ever been, even in my nightmares."

Eight months after the accident, I learned that ketamine infusions had been shown to alleviate treatment-resistant depression like mine in 60 to 70 percent of patients. I only knew ketamine as a notorious hallucinogenic party drug, but the FDA had recently approved its use for treating mood disorders.

A 60 to 70 percent success rate seemed like a good bet.

With Dr. Rosen's hesitant approval, I booked an appointment at a ketamine clinic in San Francisco, where I filled out a multi-page disclaimer before trailing a nurse to a small room with a reclining chair. She turned on some bland spa music and found my vein on the first poke—a good omen—and let the ketamine flow. I was worried that I'd have a bad trip, but the opposite occurred. My mind drifted through a magical realm of rainbow-colored fractals, infinitely complex geometric shapes that repeat in a never-ending pattern, and I melted away entirely. After each of my six forty-five-minute sessions, I wished I could live in the ketamine glow forever.

But a few days after my last treatment, the glow dissipated and my depression came roaring back, followed in full force by the same flu-like symptoms I'd suffered for years. Nobody told me that brain injuries cause neuroinflammation, which can exacerbate preexisting immune disorders like mine.

How could no one have mentioned that? Did they not read my medical history?

Trying to explain the depth of my misery to friends and family was an exercise in futility.

"So . . . you feel tired?" they asked sympathetically.

"More than tired," I'd answer, trying not to sound irritated. "Sometimes I can barely get out of bed." Although tired didn't even begin to cover how I felt, it was—and sometimes still is—the simplest explanation.

I didn't mention my fragile mental health. It was easier for people to understand physical pain. And not wanting to be a Debbie Downer, I reassured them: "I have a lot of doctors working on this, so I'm sure I'll be better soon!"

In truth, everything was a slog. I peeled myself out of bed to teach my class at San Quentin only because thirty-five men depended on me. I forced myself to go to the grocery store only because I needed to eat. I didn't do things for pleasure anymore—I was merely checking items off an endless to-do list so I could climb back into bed and pull the covers over my head.

Dr. Rosen prescribed a different antidepressant, Lexapro, and I waited impatiently for it to kick in. I rarely left home and had stopped going to social events. When friends texted to invite me to coffee, I'd text back that I was "out of town." Which was ironic. Unable to attend Parents' Weekend at Isobel's college, visit my aging parents in Vermont, or take our annual road trip with Susanne's family to Lake Siskiyou, in far Northern California, near Mt. Shasta, I felt as though I was disappointing everyone I most loved.

January 2019 – October 2020

About a year after the accident, I stumbled across the website of a clinic in Austria. The clinic promoted "biological medicine," which assessed potential imbalances in the body. I liked the idea of supporting my body naturally, and one sentence in particular caught my attention: "*We can offer almost all patients hope and progress, even in difficult cases.*"

After my experience in the Bahamas, I made sure I did due diligence this time. The clinic, which was founded in 1945, had been featured in mainstream news. I was especially intrigued by a therapy called "whole body hyperthermia," also known as "fever therapy," which uses extreme heat to kill pathogens. The idea was to simulate a fever, which kick-starts the immune system. And although I still had no clue whether pathogens were the root cause of my suffering, it seemed as good a place to continue as any.

I had drained my savings account of tens of thousands of dollars pursuing other treatments not covered by insurance, however, and was strapped for cash. I reluctantly phoned my parents. At fifty-seven, I felt like a child again asking them for money, but they'd always been tremendously supportive of me. Back when they thought I had MS, they made generous donations to the Multiple Sclerosis Foundation. Lyme was also something easy for them to understand because they lived on the East Coast, where tick-borne diseases are a constant threat. But as my diagnoses became messier, they were as confused as I was. Nonetheless, they were happy to help financially.

Three weeks later, I arrived in Austria. The modern white clinic nestled in the rolling emerald hills just outside of Vienna offered sweeping vistas of a beautiful lake. Everything exuded health, peace, and cleanliness: The pristine views of nature, the rosy-cheeked staff in their crisp white uniforms, the unblemished white orchids lining the counters. I relaxed into the beauty of my surroundings, hoping I'd find the answer to what ailed me.

The hyperthermia treatment, however, was anything but peaceful. After donning a hospital gown and climbing into a coffin-like chamber, my body was heated to 103 degrees. It was as if I were being boiled alive in my own sweat. For two hours, I focused on my breath and meditated, forcing myself to remain still and not scream for the attendant to let me out. Afterward, I was completely wrung out and took a cab back to the hotel, where I slept the sleep of the dead for twelve hours between stiff white sheets.

I spent a month at the clinic, alternating between three-times-a-week fever treatments, IV infusions of vitamins and supplements, and consulting with nutritionists.

By the end of my stay, however, I was no better. My sickness and severe depression persisted throughout the trip; the Lexapro wasn't working. I flew back to California feeling utterly defeated. I'd been riding a roller coaster of excitement and disappointment for years, but hope was slowly but surely eroding.

Would I ever feel normal again?

When I arrived home and walked through the door, Nunu gave me a huge hug. She had dinner waiting and put Isobel on the speakerphone as we sat at the kitchen table. They were excited to hear about my trip and pelted me with questions. I forced my voice to remain neutral; I knew how eager my daughters were to have a healthy mom.

"I don't know if it's working yet," I said, "but it's great to be back home again."

And so, I rallied—again. I had to. For my family. For myself.

A few months after my return from Austria, I googled "chronic illness," "treatment," and "help." Most of the results focused on accepting a diagnosis of chronic disease.

Accept? Nope. I'm not throwing in the towel. My DNA comes from tough Swedes and pull-yourself-up-by-your-bootstraps New Englanders. I'm going to beat this thing.

Though Dr. Mossman had done his best, after five years of little improvement, I needed to find someone new. Someone who could make me better for good. I returned to the online discussion boards and up popped the name of Dr. Kurtz, a local doctor who specialized in chronic illness.

Three weeks later, I drove across the bay to Dr. Kurtz's Berkeley office. He was a stocky man with shaggy blond hair and a prominent brow, and he wore John Lennon glasses perched on the tip of his nose. We spent an hour reviewing my medical history, and when I told him about the failed treatment in Austria, he shook his head sympathetically. "I haven't known anyone personally who's been helped there."

And there it was. For every diagnosis there was always someone to dismiss it and suggest a different one. For every proposed treatment, someone else to scoff at its effectiveness and promote yet another.

Dr. Kurtz ordered blood tests to check for genetic defects and environmental toxins, as well as an extensive set of dental X-rays to look for undiagnosed infections. He scrolled through the mycotoxin report that I'd received from Dr. Mossman and groaned.

"I know and respect Dr. Mossman, but this borders on malpractice. I believe he misinterpreted the report, which clearly shows that you have remarkably high levels of toxic mold in your body."

The symptoms of toxic mold exposure, as he explained them, seemed uncannily familiar: exhaustion, nausea, brain fog, night sweats, and headache—exactly what I'd been experiencing on and off for almost twenty-five years. Once again, I leapt at the possibility of an answer to my enigmatic disease. The more Dr. Kurtz explained, the more sense it made. *Stachybotrys chartarum*, a black mold that produced harmful toxins called mycotoxins, was a common problem in the Bay Area's often-damp climate of foggy summers and rainy winters.

With renewed hope, I began using the anti-mold nasal sprays he prescribed. But an hour later, my nose would bleed and waves of nausea left me gagging over the toilet. We then tried a different approach: anti-mold medication and a series of twenty IV drips containing natural antioxidants, including glutathione, phosphatidylcholine, and folinic acid to repair damaged cells and my immune system. The cocktail of antioxidants was similar to the Viva Regimen that hadn't helped me in 2016, but I hoped it might be different enough to be beneficial.

Twice a week I drove to Dr. Kurtz's clinic, where I sat in a recliner for an hour, listening to a podcast or deleting emails while antioxidants dripped into my veins. After ten weeks, however, I'd seen no improvement. At our next appointment, I forced myself to stay calm as Dr. Kurtz suggested that the IV treatment hadn't worked because there was toxic mold growing *inside* my home.

"As long as there's mold in your house, you won't get better," he said.

Oh, Lord have mercy.

"But Dr. Mossman already had me test for exposure in my house," I protested. "The plates he gave me showed minimal levels of toxic mold."

Dr. Kurtz's face twisted in horror. "Those do-it-yourself petri dish tests are highly inaccurate! You need a professional to come to your home and conduct a visual inspection and more sophisticated tests." He jotted down the name of a local mold expert, known casually as a mold sniffer.

I spent the next week squinting at crevices in my floors and walls, wondering if they were hiding armies of black spores. Despite the winter chill, I kept the windows open, hoping fresh air would dissipate the invisible menace. When Sam, the mold sniffer, showed up, he treated my house as if it were a crime scene. Wearing elbow-length gloves and a mask, he wiped down surfaces with white pads that he tucked into plastic bags. I lay on the sofa, listening to him move from room to room. After an hour, he gave me his grim diagnosis.

"I suspect there's mold in some of the walls," he said. "But we'll know more after we get the lab results."

The report confirmed his suspicions: "The main level of the house has 'very high' levels of *Stachybotrys*. But all three floors are infested with a cross contamination of *A. fumigatus, A. flavus, A. penicillioides,* and *P. brevicompactum*, and others."

As I read the report on my laptop, sunlight slanted through the windows onto the pine floors, making the house feel warm and welcoming. Yet it appeared that with every breath, I was inhaling invisible toxins. I jumped off the sofa and rushed to the front door, threw it open, and sat on my front step, trying not to hyperventilate. I wasn't just worried about myself, but also about my girls.

Sam's plan of attack included tearing walls down to the studs in three rooms, replacing wood floors with tile, and installing new carpet and airtight windows. I would have to vacate the house for six months, which meant packing everything up, moving it to storage, and finding a furnished apartment in a newly constructed building that was less likely to have mold issues.

How in the name of God am I going to do all of that when I'm so damn sick?

"Should I just sell the house and move to Arizona?" I was only half kidding.

Sam laughed. "Well, you'd still have to get rid of the mold before anyone would consider buying your house. And even if you moved to a drier climate, there's no guarantee against leaky pipes."

A group of friends rallied to help Nunu pack up the house. I was so mentally and physically exhausted that I'd collapsed amidst the boxes in tears. Each day, Nunu helped me to the sofa, where I did my best to supervise from flat on my back. I was as sick and depressed as I'd ever been, but if tearing apart my house would end this nightmare, so be it.

For the next six months, I woke up each day in my mycotoxin-free rental apartment expecting to feel better, only to be crushed by a familiar wave of fatigue. I did the bare minimum: driving Nunu back and forth to school, keeping my San Quentin program afloat, and waiting for things to improve.

When Nunu and I moved back into our renovated home, we stepped into the living room, and I took in the freshly painted walls and new carpets.

The house is fixed. And now I'll be fixed, too.

A month passed. Two months. Three. I was just as sick as ever. And to add insult to injury, my insurance company, after reimbursing me for the mold remediation, refused to renew my policy.

I sent Dr. Kurtz a message through his online patient portal.

"I'm really feeling desperate," I wrote. "I'm still sick after all the work

I did at my house. What else can we do?"

When he called me back, he did his best to reassure me. "We have to assume there is still mold in your body. Now that the house is clean, it should be easier to get rid of it."

Here we go again . . .

Dr. Kurtz prescribed an injectable peptide to reduce inflammation, another oral antifungal medication, and several more supplements. He rambled on about the new protocol, using medical jargon that I didn't understand. I was too tired to ask him to explain.

While I continued my battle with what I'd been told was toxic mold, I was also still struggling with major depression. After the ketamine and Lexapro failed, I went back to Dr. Rosen, who prescribed more traditional antidepressants—Paxil, Nuedexta, Trintellix, and Fetzima. Each time I started a new medication, I'd have to wait six weeks for it to kick in. Some of the drugs made me anxious, others left me feeling more depressed, and still others had no effect whatsoever.

"Hang in there!" Dr. Rosen chirped. "We'll find the right one eventually."

But we didn't find the right one. As we ran low on options, he suggested transcranial magnetic stimulation (TMS), which used magnetic pulses to jump-start the brain synapses that regulate mood. He told me that more than 80 percent of patients had seen their depression lift after TMS. Although I hadn't fallen into 60 to 70 percent of patients helped by ketamine, an 80 percent success rate sounded much better. The therapy consisted of thirty-six TMS sessions. Thankfully, unlike most of the other treatments I'd pursued, they were covered by insurance.

Five days a week, for the next six weeks, I lowered myself into yet another recliner where Dr. Rosen secured my head in a brace, then placed a curved wand containing electromagnetic coils against my left prefrontal cortex.

During the forty-minute sessions, I heard sharp clicks and felt an uncomfortable tapping sensation on my skull, like a fleet of tiny hammers. I consoled myself by visualizing the magnets piecing the injured parts of my brain back together.

I continually asked myself, "Do I feel better?" and, if I did, "How long will it last?" Sometimes I woke in the morning feeling a bit lighter, but by afternoon despair would grip me again.

Be patient. Dr. Rosen said it could take up to a month to work.

After two months, it was clear that I was among the unlucky 20 percent of people for whom TMS had no effect. I feared that my brain had been permanently damaged, and that nothing would help.

It's hard to describe severe depression, which is neither psychic pain nor existential pain. It's physical pain, pure and simple—a fact backed by neuroscience studies showing that psychological pain and physical pain activate the same regions of the brain. In short, pain is pain.

But those who've never experienced severe depression mistakenly believe that you can get over it by "focusing on the positive." As if depression were something we choose to indulge in or is a character flaw. No one would ever tell someone suffering from kidney stones to just "smile more." The brain is an organ like any other, and the physical damage my brain sustained in the accident caused my depression.

The next time I saw Dr. Rosen, he was compassionate but seemed to be grasping at straws.

"Let's try Prozac again," he said.

"But it didn't work the first time," I countered. It was all I could do not to snap at him.

"Then let's add in a bit of Adderall, a stimulant, to see if that helps."

I pressed my lips together and looked away to mask my irritation. It was as if he were improvising a soup recipe, throwing in a bit of this, a dash of that, and making it up as he went along. It was becoming increasingly clear that he was unsure how—or even if—he could help me.

A week later, a childhood friend came to San Francisco for a conference and invited me to dinner. I hadn't seen her in a decade, so I put on clean clothes, brushed my hair, and dragged myself to the Chinatown restaurant where we'd arranged to meet. My plan was to duck out after an hour or so. Over shared plates of pot stickers and hand-pulled noodles, we recalled our teenage exploits in New York City: seeing Elton John at Madison Square Garden for our first concert, smoking pot for the first time, and defying our parents by sneaking into a movie theater to see *The Exorcist*.

She filled me in on her successful legal career, happy marriage, and exotic travels. When it was my turn, I summarized my ongoing medical drama; it was too exhausting to give the full rundown. She peppered me with questions, and while I could see that she was concerned about me, it was clear she couldn't understand why my symptoms were so incapacitating.

"So, what, *exactly*, do you have?"

I took a deep breath and tried again to explain, but she cut me off.

"I get all that, but what's the actual *diagnosis*?"

"Well, it's kind of complicated," I said. As I launched into my decades-long history of misdiagnoses and treatments, she sat back in her chair and narrowed her eyes. I sensed a whiff of judgment, as if she were trying to figure out whether I was a hypochondriac. I found myself talking both faster and louder, as if more words and greater volume would convince her that my experiences were real.

Her eyes glazed over.

If one of my oldest friends doesn't believe me, who will? I was teetering on the edge of despair.

I left the restaurant frustrated and angry. "Try living in my body for a week, bitch, then maybe you'll get it," I muttered as I gunned my car out of the parking lot.

Driving back over the Golden Gate Bridge toward Marin, I was overwhelmed by a sudden urge to pull over and jump—to end my misery. Lord knows I wouldn't have been the first. People from around the world have made their way to the iconic red bridge to end their lives, with some two thousand jumping into the waters below since it opened in 1933.

My heart pounding, I tapped my brakes and glanced into my rear-view mirror. Traffic was light this late at night. It would be easy to get out of the car and climb over the railing.

Which direction should I face? The dark immensity of the Pacific Ocean? Or the shining lights of the city I love?

Headlights blazed behind me, and I instinctively pressed the gas pedal and sped home. I was horrified; I couldn't believe what I'd almost done. When I arrived back at the house, I called Dr. Rosen's private emergency line.

"I almost jumped off the Golden Gate Bridge just now," I told him, my voice cracking as the tears began to flow. "I don't want to die, but I can't keep living like this. I think it's time to try ECT."

Thank God Nunu is with Bob tonight. She doesn't need to hear this.

Dr. Rosen agreed immediately. He had mentioned electroconvulsive treatment (ECT) in previous conversations, but we'd agreed that it was a treatment of last resort. Much of what I knew about ECT came from the scene in the movie *One Flew Over the Cuckoo's Nest*, when Jack Nicholson's character is forcibly held down and shocked, his agonized grimace filling the screen.

After confirming that I was well enough to drive, Dr. Rosen told me to go straight to a nearby psychiatric hospital.

"Go the emergency room and tell them you're suicidal," he instructed. "It's the only way to be admitted."

As I sped down the freeway, I kept thinking about Nicholson's convulsing body, but Dr. Rosen had assured me that ECT was now done under general anesthesia.

When I arrived at the hospital, I sat for a while in the parking lot, working up the nerve to get out of the car.

How the hell have I come to this?

My legs trembling, I made my way to the ER entrance. The hospital's sliding doors whooshed open, and I walked over to the young woman behind the registration desk. I stared at her, struggling to get the words out.

"My doctor . . . " I began, unsure what to say next. She nodded encouragingly, waiting for me to continue. "My doctor told me to come here. I'm feeling suicidal."

"You came to the right place," she said kindly. I took the clipboard of forms she handed me, my hands shaking, and turned to find a seat. It was almost 11 p.m., but the waiting room was nearly full.

I'd filled out so many of these forms over the years, endlessly repeating my symptoms, medications, and failed treatments—pages and pages documenting the fact that nothing had helped me. After returning the clipboard to the receptionist, I sat down on one of the hard plastic chairs in a corner of the room. I bent forward over my knees, letting my long hair curtain my face, and began to cry. I was dimly aware of the woman sitting next to me gently rubbing my back, but by the time I was composed enough to thank her, she was gone.

I gradually became aware of my surroundings—the glaring lights, the family of five talking over each other next to me, the wailing of a baby.

How long have I been here?

I fished my phone from my bag and tapped the screen. It was almost midnight, so nearly an hour. I swiped the screen and an "On This Day 15 years ago" photo notification appeared. It was a picture of my daughters and me playing Candy Land on the living room floor. We were laughing, enjoying one of those ordinary yet special moments of family life.

How can I tell my girls that their mother is about to admit herself to a psych ward?

Forty-five minutes later, a nurse with two long braids led me to a curtained-off bed in the emergency department. She stood outside the curtain as I slipped into a hospital gown and waited as I shoved my clothes and purse into a plastic bag labeled "Patient Belongings." When I was done, she verified my name before snapping a hospital ID bracelet around my wrist.

A man called out a greeting, then swished the curtain aside. "I'm Dr. Matheson," he said, pulling the curtain closed behind him. His baby-butt-smooth skin told me he was a medical resident. "So, what brings you in tonight?"

Do I have to repeat it all again? Why don't you just read the damn intake form?

I balled my hands into fists and burst into tears. The nurse had gone, and he stood awkwardly beside my bed. Finally, I choked out the words: "I'm suicidal and I need help."

"Okay," he said, uncertainly. "I'll be right back."

He left—probably to consult with more experienced colleagues—and returned thirty minutes later to say he'd ordered routine tests: a urinalysis, an EKG, and a blood draw. I guessed he was checking my pee for drugs. A few minutes later, the nurse bustled in with a tray of shiny instruments and wrapped an orange rubber tourniquet above my right elbow.

"Make a fist," she said, tapping the inside of my forearm. She jabbed me with the needle but couldn't find a vein. Rather than start over, she jammed the needle from side to side, trying to find a way in even as I squirmed in pain. By this point, my veins were scarred from more than a hundred blood draws and IV treatments.

"Try the left arm," I whispered. "It's less scarred." She looked at me sharply, probably assuming I was a junkie. I didn't have the energy to set her straight.

After the nurse left, I lay on my back, closing my eyes against the glare of the fluorescent lights overhead. I heard muttering coming from behind other curtained-off beds, an occasional whimper, and voices over the PA system calling doctors to various wards.

Around 2 a.m., an orderly pushing an empty wheelchair arrived and told me they'd found a bed for me in the psychiatric unit. He moved to help me into the chair, but I pulled my arm away. "I'm perfectly capable of walking," I said.

"Sorry, ma'am, it's hospital policy."

A security guard stood behind him, his face impassive. The orderly pushed my chair down a long corridor, the guard following closely behind. I was surprised by his presence, but realized that, as a psych patient, I was considered unpredictable and potentially dangerous. We rode the elevator to the third floor in silence, then turned down another long hallway before stopping in front of a set of locked metal doors. The guard swiped a key card, and the doors swung open to reveal a nurses' station, where the orderly handed over my paperwork.

One of the nurses joined our little party, leading us to a darkened room with two curtained-off beds. The one next to the window was already occupied, and in the dim light that spilled into the room from the hallway, I saw the curtain move.

After the nurse left, I tossed and turned on the stiff hospital mattress, trying to sleep. I was beginning to drift off when the patient on the other side of the room began to shriek.

"I'm not goddamn crazy!" she shouted. "*He's* crazy as shit!" There was a sound of metal clanging against metal—I assumed she was handcuffed to the bed rail—and then, "Get me the hell out of here!"

Two nurses rushed in and disappeared behind the curtain, murmuring and cajoling. They must have given the woman a sedative because she dialed down the volume.

I'd fallen into a fitful sleep when she started up again. "Let me out of here!" she shrieked. "I'm not crazy!" The attendants returned, once again murmuring, cajoling, and, presumably, sedating.

This cycle repeated several times. Wrung out with exhaustion, nausea, and a pounding headache, I couldn't take it anymore and called out for help.

"Excuse me!"

A nurse swept into my space. "Yes?"

"I can't sleep like this," I said. "Isn't there another room?"

"There aren't any other beds available. I'm sorry."

"Then could you at least give me something to knock me out?" My voice sounded ragged.

She gave me 25 mg of Atarax, but it didn't help. My unseen roommate continued to mutter and shout.

An hour later, I rang the nurses' station and was given 3 mg of melatonin. That didn't make a dent either.

At 3:00 in the morning I rang again. This time, I was offered chamomile tea.

"I don't need *tea*. Please just get me away from the screaming."

Again, I was told there were no beds available. Finally, around 4:30 a.m., I stumbled down the corridor in tears, and a kind nurse who didn't look a day over twelve took pity on me and helped me drag my mattress to the day room. She covered me with a blanket and sat with me until daylight, when we dragged the mattress back to my room. My roommate was still cursing a blue streak.

After finishing my breakfast of scrambled eggs, I hit the call button, hoping that someone on the day shift would be able to find me a quieter room. A severe-looking nurse in her forties entered, and I worried that the night nurse might have told her I'd been uncooperative.

"Good morning," I said, mustering just enough energy to sound cheerful. "Is there any way I could move to a new room today?"

"Sorry, we're at full capacity," she said. "Anything else?"

I was angry and feeling increasingly desperate, but I caught myself, realizing I needed to watch my tone to avoid being labeled belligerent. I asked to see my chart, curious to know what the resident had written about me. The nurse hesitated, but by law she had no choice. She left to get it, and upon her return, she handed it to me wordlessly. I flipped it open to read the intake form signed by the ER physician.

Diagnosis: Severe recurrent major depression without psychotic features

Given the patient's acute psychiatric decompensation . . . the patient warrants inpatient psychiatric admission for stabilization, psychiatric workup, treatment adjustment, and transitional care planning.

The patient is willing to come into the hospital on a voluntary basis . . . but will require urgent psychiatric evaluation for 5150 if she were to attempt to leave AMA.

Given my bone-crushing depression, "acute psychiatric decompensation" sounded about right. It took a while to decipher the rest. A "5150" permitted a legal seventy-two-hour emergency psychiatric hold—involuntary hospitalization for someone considered a danger to themselves or others. AMA was the acronym for attempting to leave a hospital "against medical advice." In lay language, it meant that if I left the hospital without a doctor's permission, they could hold me against my will.

Well, that's sobering.

I was wheeled to my first ECT the next morning before breakfast and climbed onto a padded table. On the ceiling above was a poster of an idyllic white sand beach with two Adirondack chairs and the word BEACH in blue lettering. I'm sure it was meant to encourage patients to relax, but my body was tense with fear. The nurse attached electrodes to my chest to monitor my heart, and to my scalp to measure my brain's electrical activity. She explained that the electrodes on my head would emit a current that would cause a brief seizure, but that I wouldn't feel a thing.

As she inserted a needle into my forearm to start a saline IV drip, a blue-garbed doctor strode in. He introduced himself and announced that it was time to put me under. The anesthesia burned in my veins as the nurse wedged a rubber bite guard into my mouth and covered the lower half of my face with an oxygen mask. The last thing I saw before I went under was BEACH.

I woke up in the recovery room, woozy and disoriented. The doctor came in a few minutes later. He looked pleased and told me I'd had a "good seizure," whatever that meant.

During the ten days I was in the hospital, Bob, Nunu, Susanne, and a few other close friends came to visit. Thankfully, my shrieking roommate had gone. I forced myself to be cheerful, particularly with Nunu, who looked worried. I reached for her hand and assured her I was getting better and would be home soon.

The ECT seemed to work, at least at first. After the fourth session, the constant dread that had hollowed me out for months started to lift. I was discharged to continue the treatments at a hospital closer to home. I never wanted to see the inside of that place again.

For the next four months, I underwent ECT three times a week. Sometimes I woke up from the general anesthesia with nausea or a dull post-seizure headache—a small price to pay, I figured, to escape the abyss of depression. But while I occasionally noticed a slight shift in my mood after treatments, as the months passed, there was no consistent relief, and I found myself sinking more deeply into despair.

When I broached the subject with my ECT doctor, she was vague, saying results depended on the individual. I turned to Google and was alarmed to discover there was a danger of significant memory loss from electroconvulsive therapy. In addition, and even more worrisome, studies showed that the average number of ECT sessions needed to lift treatment-resistant depression like mine was between six and ten. I'd had twenty-seven treatments, with more scheduled.

Is anybody paying attention to this but me?

I canceled the next treatment and met with my doctor instead. "This isn't working," I told her, my words spilling out in a rush. "All the studies I've read say that most people feel better after six to ten treatments. I've had twenty-seven and I'm not getting results."

She seemed surprised by my outburst, and I could see her trying to figure out what to say.

"It's your call," she said awkwardly. "What do *you* think you should do?"

I stared at her. *If I had the answer I wouldn't be here, lady.*

When I finally spoke, I heard the desperation in my voice. "Is there any other treatment you can think of? Anything at all?"

She tapped an index finger against her lips. "Hmmm. Well, there *is* an epilepsy drug used off-label for depression. Lamotrigine. It's in a different class of medications from the antidepressants you took before."

She knew I'd taken over a dozen different antidepressants and that all of them had failed, as had the ketamine and transcranial magnetic stimulation.

I drove to Walgreens to collect the prescription, then race-walked back to my car, where I sat behind the wheel and gathered enough saliva to swallow one of the large triangular white pills. I knew from experience that antidepressants took up to six weeks to kick in, so I resigned myself to gutting out the wait. There was no other choice.

After three days of taking Lamotrigine, however, I sat up in bed and realized I felt different. I felt . . . better. I usually found the morning sun that streamed through my bedroom window oppressive—the start of another dreary day when all I craved was the oblivion of night. But now the morning light struck me as lovely, even cheerful.

I just woke up feeling happy!

A bird launched into song from the Monterey pine off the deck and I listened with joy instead of pulling the pillow over my ears. I was hungry, so I padded barefoot downstairs, grabbing a handful of strawberries from the refrigerator and switching on the coffee machine. I sat at the kitchen table and looked out at a camellia bush on my deck, which despite my neglect, was bursting with pale pink blossoms.

Wow. This must be what it feels like to return from the dead.

It was as if I had emerged from hibernation. Although I was occasionally down with the old flu-like symptoms, I pushed through and for the most part felt well enough to jump back into life: I joined a women's book club and a hiking group, savored dinners with friends, signed up for a pottery class, and returned—happily—to the classroom at San Quentin.

Just as I was reemerging into life, however, a deadly virus was sweeping the globe. In March, a stay-at-home order closed all California schools and shuttered nonessential businesses. The prison was under strict quarantine and my program was suspended indefinitely. Isobel flew home from college, and she and Nunu logged into Zoom classes from their bedrooms.

The three of us made the best of being housebound, though we sometimes got on each other's nerves, arguing over whose turn it was to empty the dishwasher or fill the gas tank. I planted a garden for the first time since I'd been hit by the car, patting cherry tomatoes and zucchini seedlings into the dirt. It was nourishing to feel my hands in the soil again. I also added two more fluffy baby chicks to our flock.

Even as I nurtured life in my yard, COVID was doing the opposite on a global scale, and the death toll continued to climb. Then, in May, a Minneapolis police officer killed George Floyd, sparking worldwide outrage. The girls and I masked up to join thousands of other protestors marching down Market Street in San Francisco. After being isolated for so long, it was exciting to be out in the world and involved with such an important cause, but after a few blocks I grew tired and turned back to wait for the girls in the car.

When Nunu finished high school in June, COVID precautions preempted a traditional graduation; a drive-by ceremony was held instead. A few weeks later, after we'd all tested negative for COVID, the girls and I joined Susanne and her daughters on our annual pilgrimage to Lake Siskiyou, where we hiked and swam in the clean crystal water.

But even as we vacationed in the California wilderness, wildfires hundreds of miles away were destroying other regions. In July, the smoke from half a million burning acres across the state converged above the Bay Area to create an eerie, dark orange blanket. We spent a couple of days under an apocalyptic sky, texting worried friends and family to let them know we were safe. Concerned about the effect of the dense smoke on our health, I bought several air purifiers, switching them on to the highest setting.

Between the pandemic, the raging fires, and the global protests against police brutality, 2020 should have been a year to hunker down in the safety of hearth and home. But I felt halfway decent for the first time in years and was restless, practically vibrating with wanderlust. The world shut down just as I was ready to live again.

International travel was out of the question, but what about a cross-country road trip? Route 66 had enticed me since I was a teenager, conjuring up images of the biker movie *Easy Rider* and the thrill of hitting the road with no particular destination in mind. Route 66 was a living remnant of my favorite decade, the sixties, when carloads of hippies fled middle America for the Golden State, landing in communes and on the streets of San Francisco's Haight-Ashbury district, where they celebrated freedom with love-ins and be-ins, and forged new paths for themselves.

In 1973, as a fifteen-year-old Brooklynite at the tail end of the hippie era, I'd once sneaked out to attend a "smoke-in" in Greenwich Village with hundreds of other young people in jeans and cutoff shorts who lounged on woven blankets, strumming guitars and sharing joints. I fit right in with my bell bottoms, Gloria Steinem aviator glasses, and long straight hair parted in the middle. I loved the sense of community.

Although I hadn't experienced Haight-Ashbury circa 1965, I nonetheless managed to express my inner hippie by plastering the bumper of my Honda minivan with anti-war and feminist stickers. I hoped that by traveling down the patchouli-scented pavement of Route 66, I could recapture a bit of the soaring sense of freedom I'd soaked up in Greenwich Village and, later, at Burning Man.

I talked Lisa, a college friend, into being my road buddy. At eighteen, we'd lived in the same Kenyon College dorm and were both on the swim team. I'd always been envious of the way Lisa knifed through the water like a machine, even when she was hungover. Forty years after our freshman year, we were both sixty-two, divorced with grown kids, and eager to bust out of our quarantined lives.

With the help of travel guides and a large spiral-bound atlas, I mapped out our trip with a yellow highlighter. Eighteen fun-loving days traveling coast to coast. Lisa would fly to California from her home in Connecticut and we'd drive back East, stopping at iconic sites along the way. There were several times when one of us almost backed out of the trip—COVID was still raging, and a vaccine had yet to be released—but we decided that if we took strict precautions, we could make the trip about as safe as an outing to the grocery store. We would wear masks in public and avoid restaurants, keeping a cooler stocked with food in the trunk. I volunteered to be the one to breach our hotel rooms first, armed with an N95 mask and a spray bottle of rubbing alcohol.

At the beginning of October, I picked Lisa up from the airport in a rented Toyota SUV. Our plan was to head south down the California coast, cross into Arizona, pass through New Mexico and the Texas panhandle, and swing up to the Ozarks, before leaving Route 66 to cut across Tennessee and up through the Appalachian Mountains.

In the Mojave Desert, we pulled over on the side of a dirt road for a pee break and were surprised by how the desert, which looked monochromatic from a distance, was so startlingly colorful up close. Tiny pink flowers blanketed the sand, and orange and gold mineral striations lined the rock faces. We just had to slow down to notice.

It was a first visit for both of us to the Grand Canyon, which was more magnificent than we'd ever imagined: the bright blue sky, the red and orange canyon cliffs, the sound of white sage crunching under our hiking boots, the sun-dazzled green needles of the pinyon pines. After a mile of hiking down the grueling switchbacks of the Bright Angel trail, Lisa turned back. I forged ahead for another mile, propelled by my renewed health. I enjoyed a moment of smug satisfaction: I was the strong one that afternoon, and Lisa was swimming in the slow lane.

On the night we drove into Tucumcari, New Mexico, we were greeted by a field of flashing neon signs, remnants of the road's cross-country-car-trip heyday. At the Cadillac Ranch outside Amarillo, Texas, we stopped to take in the ten vintage Cadillacs buried nose-down in the dirt and covered in graffiti. We hadn't packed spray paint, so we used a stick to carve our initials into the rear fender of a 1963 Sedan de Ville.

We entered Memphis blasting Paul Simon's *Graceland.* Visiting Elvis's mansion was like opening a back door to the 1970s. His white patent leather ankle boots were parked next to an oversized chair, as if the King had just removed them to put his feet up.

After long days on the road, crooning along to Willie Nelson's "On the Road Again" or listening to an audiobook murder mystery, we'd pull into a motel and fall into bed. Along the way, we talked about life—our regrets, our desires, our hopes. Just two former eighteen-year-olds looking back at life and forward to the future.

I flew home triumphantly, wearing a hot pink Route 66 t-shirt. Although we'd driven across the country in a roomy SUV and not on one of the slick choppers Dennis Hopper and Peter Fonda rode in *Easy Rider*, I'd reveled in the same sense of freedom and adventure. I felt truly alive.

Memories of the trip would bolster me during the dark days to come.

November 2020 – July 2021

Back in California, I felt well enough to hit the southern Marin trails twice a week with my hiking group. There were only eight of us, so we could safely socialize outdoors. I felt strong as I climbed the redwood-studded hills, often passing slower hikers.

For years, I'd fantasized about summiting Mt. Tamalpais, and with this group I finally did. The narrow switchbacks were so steep in places that I resorted to climbing on all fours. But I made it to the top of the 2,500-foot-summit on a crystal-clear afternoon. I spun in circles, taking in the panoramic view: Beyond the emerald hills of Marin lay the turquoise blue waters of the bay. In the distance, San Francisco's skyscrapers pierced the blanket of fog that shrouded the city. A gentle breeze cooled my sweat-soaked body. I lifted my arms in triumph and announced, "I feel so damn good!" My hiking buddies grinned at me.

You have no idea.

I had been toying with the idea of getting another dog, and as I drove home after the hike, I decided it was time. Annie had died shortly after

Isobel was born, and I relished the idea of a canine companion and hiking buddy. A few weeks later, I brought home Alice, a small apricot Poodle mix. She was only twelve weeks old and not a bit housetrained. I wiped up a lot of pee and spent hours teaching her basic commands. In return, she gave me unconditional love, curling up next to me in bed and prancing behind me as I moved through the house.

Although I felt physically healthy and energetic for the most part, I struggled with increasing episodes of brain fog, a common symptom of the many things I'd been diagnosed with—Lyme disease, chronic fatigue, toxic mold exposure, and a traumatic brain injury. While brain fog sounds mild, like a passing weather system, it can seriously affect focus, concentration, and memory. Over the years, I'd learned to adapt, making lists, scheduling extra time for projects, and setting multiple reminders on my phone.

One morning, as I chatted on the phone with Lisa, I glanced at the clock on the stove and suddenly recalled that I had a 10 a.m. dental cleaning. "Oh shoot! I'm late for the dentist," I told her. I grabbed my purse off the back of a chair and looked around for my phone. "Dammit, I can't find it!" I said, hurrying upstairs to see if I'd left it by my bedside charger.

"Uh . . . Diana? You're talking on your phone right now."

I lowered my hand to check—yep, there it was—and we laughed. Lisa and I were both in our sixties, after all; we were entitled to a few senior moments.

As the pandemic stretched into winter, San Quentin remained under quarantine. Inmates weren't allowed internet access, so it was impossible to simply transfer the class online. I could, however, offer it to newly released prisoners enrolled in a local community college. But the demands and distractions of life on the outside prevented many of my students from fully participating. They struggled to navigate Zoom technology while also juggling childcare and other commitments. When enrollment dropped to ten students, I canceled the class, offering to work with the remaining students individually. I'd just have to wait for the prison to open to teach again.

As the holidays approached, I hoped to make the girls' Christmas as magical as my mother had always made it for me, so I continued many of her traditions: queuing up Sinatra on my playlist, lighting a fire in the living room, buying a big fragrant spruce, and hanging twinkling white lights throughout the house. Bob came over on Christmas morning—despite the divorce, we always celebrated the holiday as a family—and we gathered around the breakfast table and took turns sharing what we were most grateful for before moving to the living room to open gifts. I told them I was grateful for my loving family and for feeling healthy enough to fully enjoy the holidays.

I decided to ring in the 2021 New Year with an eight-mile group hike along the Dipsea Trail, which stretches from downtown Mill Valley to Stinson Beach. It's a challenging trek through steep redwood forests, grassy meadows, and hilltop ridges, so I filled my new daypack with energy bars, nuts, and apples.

A few miles in, on a downhill section of a redwood-covered slope, I began to feel the "something's wrong" exhaustion coming on and fell behind the group. I mumbled an excuse to my hiking buddies and turned back, trying not to panic as I slogged back up the hill.

Perhaps I didn't sleep as well as I thought.

I refused to entertain the possibility that this was the beginning of another downward spiral.

On the drive home, I stopped to buy groceries. I was exhausted, but we needed food for dinner. As I was lugging the bags up the front steps, I stopped short, exhausted and unable to move. The front door flew open, and Nunu, jingling her car keys, rushed out, on her way to meet friends. Seeing me hunched over, she ran down the steps toward me. I dropped the groceries—bananas, a carton of half-and-half, and several containers of yogurt tumbled down the stairs—and collapsed into her arms.

"I feel so sick!" I wailed. "Please don't let this be happening again."

It was the first time I'd cried on my daughter's shoulder instead of the other way around. Nunu helped me into the house and up to bed before retrieving the groceries. I hoped a good night's sleep would revive me, but the next morning I woke up with a pounding headache, soaked in sweat, and heavy with fatigue.

Dr. Kurtz guessed that the stress of the hike had triggered an inflammatory response and suggested we nip it in the bud with hydrocortisone and low-dose Naltrexone, a medication used to treat opioid addiction but prescribed off-label for immune disorders. I picked up the prescriptions the moment they were filled but otherwise stayed home, waiting for the drugs to kick in.

Mother of God, please, please let this work.

On January 6, Nunu and I watched the attack on the United States Capitol on TV. Between the raging pandemic, violent insurrection, and my beleaguered body, it felt as though the world was imploding—and so was I. Once again, my friends rallied to support me. Susanne indulged my sweet tooth, dropping by with ice cream and M&Ms. I couldn't really taste them, but I loved them anyway.

Over the next nine months, there were times I felt slightly better, but most of the time I suffered from overwhelming exhaustion, and it was all I could do to get through the days. Every few weeks, Dr. Kurtz adjusted dosages and added or removed supplements. He even suggested injecting peptides into my thigh again. Nothing worked.

One evening, I opened the fridge to find I was down to sour milk, five-day leftovers, and a few flaccid greens. I pulled on a coat and drove to Whole Foods to load up on prepackaged meals, doing my best to avoid eye contact with other shoppers. But as I was heading to the checkout stand, someone called out, "Diana? Is that you?"

Ugh.

I turned and saw a woman about my age who I'd known from a step class I'd taken a decade earlier. She was dressed in stylish yoga gear, her hair pulled back in a low ponytail. She looked radiant, as if she'd just stepped out of a Lululemon advertisement. I painted a smile on my face.

"Oh my gosh, I haven't seen you in *years*," she said, giving me a light hug. Pulling away, she gave me the once-over and frowned.

"Are you okay? You look . . ." Her voice trailed away.

I shifted my handbasket of frozen dinners from one hand to the other, averting my eyes. "I haven't been to the gym in a long time," I mumbled. "I've been too tired."

She put a sympathetic hand on my shoulder. "*Girl*, I have so been there."

That's when she started singing the praises of a German-born naturopath named Peter Bergmann. It turned out that she'd also struggled for years with exhaustion and misdiagnosed illnesses.

"He changed my life!" she said, a little too loudly. "I feel like a new woman!"

As soon as I got home, I googled him, of course. Dr. Bergmann's expertise was in "nutritional kinesiology," which tests muscle response to measure deficiencies in the body. I was vaguely aware of the therapy.

I was able to book an appointment that same week. Dr. Bergmann's office was in a low-slung, mixed-use building in downtown San Rafael. Beside the entrance squatted an enormous stone Buddha—which I now recognized as *de rigueur* in holistic medicine circles. A receptionist showed me to his office.

Dr. Bergmann, a man in his early fifties with wide shoulders and thinning dark hair, waved me in from behind his desk. He was reviewing the thirty-five-page intake form I'd filled out online and asked me to elaborate on some of the treatments. A shelf-lined wall held hundreds of small glass vials, beneath which sat a cabinet crowded with bottles of supplements. Another large brass Buddha—yes, there it was—meditated atop the cabinet under a wall hanging of Ganesha, the multi-armed, elephant-headed Indian god of new beginnings and wisdom.

I resented having to answer questions that I'd already responded to in written form. As I picked at my cuticles, an anxiety-driven habit I'd developed over the years, Dr. Bergmann leaned across the desk and smiled. Perhaps he sensed my irritation.

"Hang in there, Diana," he said. "The body is capable of healing itself. And your body will tell us just how to do that."

"Great, but how long will it take?" I asked wearily.

His boyish face broke into a wide smile.

"You'll feel better within three months," he said, exuding absolute confidence.

After Dr. Bergmann finished reviewing my medical history, he walked over to an illustration hanging on the wall that showed the outline of a person crisscrossed with blue lines. "This is a diagram of your body's energy system," he said. "There's an electrical circuit between the charge of the testing substance and the charge of your muscles. When we complete the circuit, that tells me what your body needs."

I winced at the talk of "energy systems," recalling my experience in the Bahamas. But he offered a different approach and came highly recommended.

Dr. Bergman plucked several vials from the shelves, explaining that they contained the electromagnetic signatures of various substances that would help him determine if I had undiagnosed nutritional deficiencies or toxicities. He placed a vial, about the size of a perfume sample, into my right hand and told me to extend my left arm parallel to the floor.

"I'm going to test your body's energetic compatibility," he said. "If your arm is strong and doesn't move when I push down on it, it's positive feedback. If it doesn't hold steady when I push, it's negative feedback." I watched him curiously, skeptical that such a simple test could tell him so much.

He repeated the test with a dozen or so vials, nodding excitedly when my arm showed weakness in response to a particular signature. He then prescribed a long list of supplements that he said would support my immune system, detoxify my liver, and control inflammation. I had taken many of them before and told him so. But he insisted that the combinations he prescribed would have a synergistic effect.

At home, I lined up the bottles on my kitchen counter and opened my laptop to delete the spreadsheet with Dr. Kurtz's pill regimen and replace it with Dr. Bergmann's supplements regimen. I tossed palmfuls of capsules into my mouth, washing them down with water. After years of taking multiple pills a day, I'd learned to master my gag reflex.

I'm giving my body what it needs to restore itself. I'm giving my body what it needs to restore itself.

After two months of seeing Dr. Bergmann twice a week for muscle testing and taking the supplements daily, I was still dragging. When I complained at my next appointment that the treatment wasn't working, he told me to be patient.

"I said it would take three months," he reminded me gently.

He then recommended a new therapy: singing and gargling. He explained that the brain injury had likely damaged my vagus nerve, a cranial nerve that stretches from the brain to the abdomen and connects to many organs.

"A damaged vagus nerve can lead to unchecked inflammation," he explained, "which could be causing your symptoms. Sing as loudly as you can to stimulate and heal the nerve."

Holy hell.

I kept a straight face in his office, but once home, I googled his odd suggestion. To my surprise, I found evidence that singing and gargling do indeed vibrate the muscles at the back of the throat and stimulate the vagus nerve.

I'll be damned.

I began to gargle with salt water twice a day and, when alone in the car, belted out a favorite disco tune, Gloria Gaynor's "I Will Survive."

Another month passed but I was still laid low with the never-ending flu-like malady. And now it seemed that the song I'd once danced to with wild abandon was mocking me. Mere survival wasn't enough. I wanted to feel normal again. But feeling normal was little more than a vague memory.

When was the last time I wasn't preoccupied with my illness? Worrying about it, managing it, trying to find the answer?

Carefree hikes in the sun and my Route 66 road trip seemed like a lifetime ago.

Early one morning, I stood at my bathroom sink staring at the three pills in my hand, trying to work up the fortitude to swallow them. Overwhelmed, I studied my reflection in the mirror, struck by how haggard I looked. Dark circles hung beneath my eyes; my hair stuck limply to my neck.

When was the last time I showered? Why am I so broken?

Isobel, who was home for the summer, yelled up the stairs, "Do we have any cereal?" I continued to stare at my reflection. Suddenly she was at my side.

"Mama, are you *okay*?"

I sat down heavily on the toilet. "I can't do this anymore," I said flatly, staring at the blue bath mat in front of me. "I can't take another day of this."

Izzy knelt in front of me and placed her hands on my knees. "Mama, don't say that! You're going to be okay!"

Oh my God . . . She thinks I'm going to kill myself.

I reached out and pulled her to my chest. "Baby, I'm not depressed anymore. The Lamotrigine is working, remember? But sometimes dealing with all my health issues is just too much."

Izzy searched my eyes, and I gave her a weak smile. "Why don't you go make us some scrambled eggs, and I'll be right down."

After she left, I gulped down the pills and went to my bedroom. As I dressed, my eyes were drawn to the greeting cards tucked into the mirror over my bureau. Over the years, my dear eighty-year-old mom had sent me a series of get-well cards, always with a red lipstick kiss on the back of the envelope. She'd written long notes of encouragement in her distinctive cursive, which often made me cry; I longed to feel her arms around me.

But this time I noticed a card sent by a friend. On the front, in bold red letters, it read, "Life can be tough. You are allowed to scream and shout. You are allowed to swear. You are allowed to cry. You are NOT allowed to give up!"

You are NOT allowed to give up.

The messages were everywhere: *Tough it out. Don't be a quitter. What doesn't kill you makes you stronger. God only gives you what you can handle.* But it was getting more and more difficult to keep a stiff upper lip.

At the end of three months, Dr. Bergmann's promised results had failed to materialize. Kinesthetic testing may indeed help people with less complex illnesses, but it hadn't helped me. I lugged three shopping bags of supplements to his office and left them outside the door, next to the Buddha. The pills were expensive, and I didn't want them to go to waste. Maybe they'd help someone else.

When COVID restrictions finally lifted that summer, my friend Linda took me to the Greek Theatre to hear the cellist Yo-Yo Ma perform. Located in the Berkeley foothills, the outdoor theater offered stunning views of the San Francisco Bay that complemented the ethereal music. What a blessed relief to be out of the house doing normal things with normal people. I forgot, for a few hours anyway, how sick I was.

I booked a cottage in Stinson Beach for a special mother-daughters trip. We walked on the beach during the day, and at night we listened to music, each of us taking turns sharing playlists. We also played round after round of Rummy 500, a card game I'd played with my family as a child—and one that we took very, very seriously. On our last night, Nunu, a natural cook, made us a dinner of roast chicken thighs drizzled with lemon juice, followed by strawberry spoon cake. I loved having my girls with me again, and for a few days, all felt warm and right with the world.

But they could tell I wasn't doing well. Long conversations drained me, and I'd lag on our beach walks. Each night, I was asleep by 9:30 p.m. I didn't feel the need to hide my misery from them anymore; they weren't little kids.

Illness is just part of who I am now.

August 2021 – February 2022

Dr. Kurtz was running out of ideas. When he suggested "switching up supplements a bit" and continuing the peptide injections, I could barely contain my frustration.

"Is there anything else—anything *new*—I can try?" I yelled.

He drummed his fingers on his desk and sighed. It was clear that he was frustrated, too. He thought for a few moments and then nodded. "There's a doctor down the hall who offers neuroenhancement. Neuroenhancement focuses on brain function that can help regulate the immune system. Maybe that's worth a try?"

A week later, I met with Dr. Mancuso, a balding man with surprisingly hairy knuckles. He studded my head with nineteen electrodes, which would record a quantitative electroencephalogram (QEEG) and reveal a map of my brain's electrical activity.

"Brain waves reveal important information about inflammation and cognition," he explained, turning his attention to the monitor beside my chair. I closed my eyes, and for the next thirty minutes, electrodes fed information from my brain into the computer.

Two days later, Dr. Mancuso emailed me a series of color-coded images of my brain, along with a summary of his findings. "The brain is showing symptoms of reduced metabolic activity, inflammation, and reduced circulation. Decrease in alpha peak frequency, which is often seen in brain injury and age-related cognitive decline. Overall, we can expect decreased efficiency in cortical processing, memory issues, and a general slowing of cognitive function."

Holy shit, this sounds just like dementia.

Jumping online, I found a National Institutes of Health article reporting that people with TBIs do, indeed, have a significantly higher risk of dementia. Trying to slow my racing thoughts, I closed my laptop and went outside to sit on the front steps. There were my chickens, happily pecking at the dirt in their coop, living their blissfully simple lives. I tilted up my head to the warm sun.

Don't jump to conclusions. But it was hard not to.

The article had also mentioned that memory problems and an inability to concentrate were two of the earliest signs of dementia—which was worrisome, because in the three years since the accident, I'd become increasingly forgetful: I'd leave the car running in the driveway or become disoriented on the way to the supermarket, the same market I'd shopped at for twenty years. Increasingly I relied on Siri to help me find my way around town. I'd sometimes be driving down the highway and realize I'd forgotten where I was headed. Writing had become more difficult, with word order an increasing mystery. I struggled to compose simple emails.

During our follow-up visit the next week, Dr. Mancuso told me that I did indeed exhibit "some early warning signs" of dementia. He rushed to assure me, however, that the weekly transcranial direct stimulation (TCDS) he was prescribing—low-level electrical stimulation of the brain, as opposed to Dr. Rosen's transcranial magnetic stimulation

(TMS), which used magnetic pulses to improve mood—could slow it down.

"Once the inflammation is under control, you should notice an improvement in both your flu-like symptoms and memory issues."

At our next appointment, Dr. Mancuso placed a small, wired sponge on either side of my forehead and switched on a current. I felt a slight tingling sensation. He sat beside me, adjusting knobs on the controller, which looked like a large TV remote.

"If it starts to sting, let me know, and I'll reduce the current," he said. But believing the stronger the better, I gripped the chair and let it sting.

Once again, Dr. Mancuso warned I might not notice immediate results.

How many times have I been told that over the years?

Over the next month, I asked myself repeatedly, *Do I have more energy? Is writing getting any easier?* It was hard to tell. But I had to believe the treatment would be successful. Any day that I woke up without a headache, I felt a glimmer of hope.

This might actually be working.

After the sixteenth treatment, Dr. Mancuso scooted his wheeled chair back from the TCDS machine and spun to face me. "That's it, our last session," he said.

"But wait, nothing's changed," I replied weakly. "I still feel terrible."

He returned his attention to the device and began shutting it down. "I *told* you it may take time to notice the effects." His voice was sharp.

Go to hell!

I grabbed my purse and got up without saying a word. As I reached the door, he spoke again, this time in a softer tone.

"Look, there's one more thing we can try."

The "one more thing" was a $1,500 helmet that used infrared light to increase blood flow, reduce inflammation, and stimulate mitochondria.

Again, I did due diligence and found studies that documented the therapeutic use of infrared light in helping to repair TBI damage.

I ordered the helmet and used it once a day for twenty minutes. Every few days, I'd find myself with a bit more energy, but it never lasted. Dr. Mancuso then told me to use the helmet twice a day, which I did for the next several months—again with no consistent results.

It was time to face the obvious: After using the helmet as many as forty minutes a day, seven days a week for five months, it had proved worthless. I threw the helmet into the back of my closet and canceled my remaining appointments.

Feeling hopeless, I spent several days in bed, hugging my pillow and wondering what bargains I'd make with God to feel better. *Would I trade an arm for good health? My vision? Would I shorten my life span by ten years to have ten solid years of health and happiness? Yes, yes, and yes.*

I had nowhere to turn but back to Dr. Kurtz, who next suggested a "chiropractic neurologist" in Berkeley. She came "highly recommended by a colleague." From the tone of his voice, it was clear he was happy to palm me off on someone else.

Dr. Greenway's website stated she specialized in many disorders including brain inflammation. After scrolling through Yelp reviews—all but one five stars—I scheduled an appointment for a few days later.

Dr. Greenway, who was in her mid-thirties and sported a sleek black pixie haircut, looked younger than she appeared in her online photo. On the wall of her waiting room hung a large sign reading, "Good Things Will Happen Today." I teared up just looking at it.

As I gave Dr. Greenway the rundown of my previous failed treatments, my voice cracked, and she reached across her desk to place her hand on mine.

"Diana, I understand how overwhelming this must be," she said, holding my gaze. "But I'm going to take very good care of you."

Tears rolled down my cheeks, and I fought an urge to crawl into her lap. She offered me a tissue and patiently waited for me to compose myself. She then walked over to a large whiteboard covered with an image of the brain.

"Here's what's going on inside your brain," she said, using a red marker to draw a series of arrows. "Traumatic brain injury destroys the glial cells, which support neurons." She drew more arrows in yellow, green, and blue. "There are three types of glial cells: Astrocytes release toxic molecules. Microglia releases inflammatory molecules. Oligodendrocytes . . ."

I struggled to follow her rapid-fire commentary. She pulled out a black marker and began drawing circles around Xs: "Laminated, lipid-rich myelin . . . action potential conduction . . . hematopoietic tissue macrophages."

Struggling to focus, I asked her to repeat everything. She did, but at the same rapid pace. "Make sense now?" she asked, pointing at me with a green marker.

I nodded, but no, it didn't.

Next, she handed me a pair of wired goggles so she could record my eye movements as I watched dots flitting around on a large monitor. "Hmm," she murmured. "Interesting."

Then she had me repeat the exercise, this time balancing on just one leg.

"Your left eye isn't tracking with your right eye," she said. "Which means the left side of your brain isn't communicating correctly with the right side of your brain."

I started to ask a question, but she told me to hold off until she was finished with her analysis. She next had me sit in a chair and keep my head immobile while I followed her thumb with my eyes. She moved her thumb up and down and side to side—not unlike what I imagined the police would do when administering a drunk-driver test.

I sat in a chair tracking her thumb three times a day—with an hour-long break between each session—three days a week for the next month. She said the exercise would help "unify" my brain. Not wanting to drive the twenty-five miles back across the bay to Mill Valley between sessions, I camped out at a nearby café during the breaks, scrolling through my phone and eavesdropping on college students complaining about course loads and bad dates.

After a month of studying Dr. Greenway's thumb—I can still picture it in my mind's eye, long and slender, its nail coated with siren-red polish—she prescribed a keto diet (high-fat, low-carb), which she said was anti-inflammatory and therefore therapeutic for brain function. She took a swipe at Dr. Kurtz for not modifying my diet earlier. "Any doctor who doesn't address diet isn't doing his job."

Each morning, I dutifully chugged down a sludgy smoothie of avocado, chia seeds, coconut cream, and whey protein powder. For once, I was happy that my sense of taste was blown.

On one of my visits, Dr. Greenway pressed a small dropper bottle into my hand—a sample of an antioxidant called glutathione, which the liver secretes to aid the immune system. I told her I'd taken glutathione via IV as part of a previous treatment and that it hadn't helped, but she told me to give it another shot.

Whatever.

At home, I verified that glutathione did indeed "help reduce the oxidative stress that causes an inflammatory response." I shrugged and tilted my head back to squeeze a few drops under my tongue, then flopped into bed to watch an episode of the BBC's *The Great Pottery Throwdown.*

After a few minutes, I noticed a peculiar sensation—as if a wave of fresh air were running over my body. I stood and walked around, feeling light on my feet for the first time in seemingly forever.

What is happening?

With each passing minute, I felt more and more energized, as if I'd been plugged into an energy source.

After spending tens of thousands of dollars chasing wellness, it's an over-the-counter supplement that's a game-changer?

I had no idea why glutathione hadn't helped before, but all that mattered was that it made me feel alive now. For the first time since my 2020 road trip, I was myself again. Aside from Lamotrigine, which stopped my depression in its tracks in December 2019, this was the first time I'd experienced an immediate positive reaction to any treatment.

Still buzzing from excitement, I emailed Dr. Greenway. "Glutathione is a MIRACLE," I wrote. I didn't want to mess with this perfect solution, so I asked for specific instructions, verifying the dosage and asking how long I should take it.

"If it worked that well," she emailed, "then probably for the rest of your life."

No problem! I stocked up, ordering ten eight-ounce bottles from an online vendor. If there was a run on glutathione, I would be safe. At least for a while.

The breakthrough couldn't have come at a better time. December 22 was my father's ninetieth birthday. I'd been feeling increasingly anxious about going, unsure if I'd have the energy to fly across the country for the celebration. Isobel and Nunu, who both lived back East, would be there, as would my brother, Mack, who was two and a half years younger. There was no better gift for Dad than having the family all together.

My dad was a perennial jokester, and when I was growing up, we played a tag-like game we called Gotcha Last. Dad would tap us on our heads and dash off, the two of us in hot pursuit. Gotcha Last carried on into adulthood, most often when we were saying goodbye—in airport terminals and bus stations, even on crowded city streets.

When my brother and I were young, my father convinced Mack that he was Superman and that when he left for his teaching job each morning, he was actually flying off to solve crimes. As I arrived home for his birthday party, my father, dressed in a Superman bodysuit, greeted me at the front door, his arms in the air.

That's my dad!

I was thrilled to feel like myself again and fully enjoy time with my family. We looked through old photo albums, cooked meals together, and laughed at my brother's stand-up comedy routines.

On the last day, as my parents waved goodbye from their doorway, I jumped out of my rental car, ran back down the driveway, and tapped Dad on the arm. "Gotcha last!" I shouted, sprinting for the car.

I felt well enough that I impulsively booked a January ski trip with Nunu. I'd been too sick to take her on college tours or help her move into her dorm at NYU, as I'd done with Isobel, and I wanted to make it up to her. More than a decade had passed since I'd been on the slopes, so I started doing squats and lunges to strengthen my quads.

After I'd been taking glutathione for about six weeks, I noticed that the effects were starting to wear off more quickly. Dr. Greenway had me increase the dosage. But then, one day, the once-magical drops stopped working altogether.

No, no, no . . . This can't be happening again.

I canceled the ski trip, disappointing Nunu and myself.

Dr. Greenway said she had no idea why the glutathione had lost its effectiveness. She mumbled something about free radicals and suggested another round of "ocular motor intensives," or as I thought of it, thumb therapy. My bullshit detector, which had been missing in action, clicked into high gear. I scoured online medical journals and learned that while ocular motor therapy was useful for brain injuries that impacted visual processing, attention, and balance, there was little to no evidence that it reduced brain inflammation.

I was so tapped out that I couldn't muster the energy to be angry at Dr. Greenway, or at Dr. Kurtz for recommending her. I directed my anger at myself instead.

How could I let myself be duped again?

Looking back, all the warning signs were there. She'd glossed over my questions with jargon-laden replies, responded with impatience when I pressed her for explanations, and in general implied that I just needed to trust her judgment because she was a doctor. Apart from the temporary glutathione fix, Dr. Greenway should have known that her "treatments" were useless for my condition. I wondered if she ever, even for a moment, questioned her integrity.

Throughout my illness, I continued to believe that people who chose to enter healing professions do so because they genuinely want to help people. That they have their patients' best interests in mind. And so I continued to put myself in their care, to trust them, and to hope.

I felt betrayed.

Once again, I was plunged into "something's wrong" tired, with all the usual symptoms. My hope that I'd ever find relief, much less a clear diagnosis, was dwindling. By this point, I'd seen dozens of doctors and spent hundreds of thousands of dollars on treatments. Nothing had brought me lasting relief from my complex and unpredictable illness. I felt utterly depleted and alone.

I don't want to feel this sick for the rest of my life.

I took to bed with my laptop, where I hung out in virtual Meetup groups filled with chronically ill people who gathered to commiserate and share advice on how to cope. The sicker people became, I'd discovered, the more they were drawn to the very fringes of alternative medicine and DIY treatments. I was on the cusp of becoming one of them.

A young woman on one of the forums mentioned finding relief with magic mushrooms. "Psychedelics are revolutionizing medicine," she told the group. Curious, I researched her claim and found several online references—including a paper on the National Institutes of Health website—claiming that psilocybin helped modulate brain inflammation and increase neuroplasticity.

I felt a familiar flicker of hope. *Maybe this is the missing key?*

Major universities, including Northwestern and Johns Hopkins, were conducting clinical trials using psilocybin to treat everything from Alzheimer's to PTSD to traumatic brain injury. I couldn't move across the country to participate in a trial, but it was relatively easy to get magic mushrooms in California. I knew someone who knew someone who'd experienced a guided psilocybin trip in a small town near mine. Given that psilocybin was illegal, when I texted the woman who would ultimately act as my guide, she asked me to correspond with her via encrypted WhatsApp messages instead.

A few weeks later, I drove an hour down the coast to meet her. The woman who opened the door—her name was Briana—wasn't the silver-haired hippie wearing a muumuu that I expected, but a young brunette with stiff posture and a personality to match. After I'd handed over an envelope stuffed with ten one-hundred-dollar bills, she led me into a living room overflowing with potted plants. I sat down on the couch, and she disappeared into the kitchen, returning a few minutes later with a small dish of dried brown mushrooms. They were gritty, tough, and hard to chew, but I choked them down and lay back on the couch. Briana covered me with a blanket and handed me a sleep mask. New Age music wafted from a speaker somewhere near my head.

"I'll be right over here," she said, sitting down in a chair on the other side of the room. Soon, a ripple of warmth and calm washed over me, similar to the sensation I'd felt while taking ketamine for depression in 2019.

I'd heard that taking mushrooms could be intense and sometimes scary but that I should "go toward" the experience, and so I did. For the next four hours, I traveled through a realm that transcended human perception and thought. There were moments when I was lucid enough to get up and go to the bathroom, but most of the time, I lay on the couch, overcome by waves of color more brilliant than anything of this world, and that carried me to a place where space and time didn't exist and a kaleidoscope of spiraling fractals unfurled in tandem with my breathing.

When my mushroom journey ended, it took a few minutes before I was ready to open my eyes. I wanted to hold on to what I'd experienced for as long as I could. I was physically and emotionally drained, but I also felt a sense of hope. Briana brought me a cup of tea and a bowl of nuts and left me to rest for a half hour until I felt ready to drive. She asked if I wanted to share my experience, but I told her I just needed to sit with it.

On the way home, I stopped for an iced latte. I was tired and needed the kick.

How long would it take for the mushrooms to work their magic on my brain and restore my health? Two weeks? A month? I messaged Briana to ask.

"I can't say," she answered. "It depends on the person. But you're welcome to come back as many times as you want."

Thanks, but a thousand dollars a pop is a lot of money for little guidance and no guarantees.

The person who hooked me up with Briana suggested another, less expensive, psychedelic therapy: micro-dosing lysergic acid diethylamide, or LSD. She connected me with a young man in the East Bay, again via an encrypted WhatsApp message, and a week later I climbed the stairs of a motel-style building to his second-floor apartment.

"There are a hundred drops in this vial," he said, handing me a small brown glass bottle. "That's a full-on trip, but for micro-dosing, you're just going to take two drops once a day. Three drops max. Any more than that and you may have a hard time functioning."

It was just thirty dollars for three vials—a bargain compared to that thousand-dollar mushroom experience.

The next morning, I put two drops under my tongue. An hour later, I started to feel a mixture of relaxed, as if time had slowed to a crawl, and hyper-aware. It was as if I'd taken a mild sedative—but also consumed a pot of coffee.

I prowled Google for data on when I might notice the brain-healing effects of LSD, but I couldn't find any. There was no credible information, only anecdotal reports posted on obscure internet forums. Micro-dosing was still very much an experimental therapy.

What if it's not even effective in cases like mine?

Turns out it wasn't. Although I took the LSD micro-dose every other morning for several months and loved how relaxed I felt, my debilitating fatigue continued unabated.

A month or so after I stopped micro-dosing LSD, someone on the chronic illness forum mentioned 5-MeO-DMT, the venomous secretion of the Sonoran Desert toad, which had been shown to spur nerve growth, support immune regulation, and control neuroinflammation.

Like magic mushrooms and LSD, it was also classified as a Schedule 1 controlled substance, but by this time, I didn't care. As my friend said, "You've done just about everything else, Diana. You've got nothing to lose."

Three weeks later, a shaman arrived at my door wearing a maroon poncho and flip-flops. He had a PhD in chemistry and had learned about healing with plant medicine from his father in Peru. I sat cross-legged on the floor of my living room as he chanted in Spanish and burned sage to cleanse the space. When he was done, he pulled a leather pouch from his poncho and extracted a pinch of white crystalline powder. He patted the powder into the bowl of a pipe, explaining that it was a synthetic compound that mimicked the secretions of the toad, which was now endangered because of increased demand for 5-MeO-DMT.

The shaman ran a lighter under the pipe. "Hold the smoke in your lungs while I count backwards from ten," he said, as the powder crackled. I followed his instructions, inhaling the sharp vapor. When he reached "one," I exhaled and fell back on the couch cushions he'd arranged behind me.

I opened my eyes thirty minutes later to the sound of a voice moaning, "I don't want to come back, I don't want to come back." It took a few moments to realize it was my own voice I was hearing.

I don't remember seeing much during my trip, but I do recall the feeling: I was connected to everyone and everything. I felt an exquisite peace as I dissolved into a brilliant light; there was no "me" anymore.

It was unbearable to return to my sick body.

The shaman helped me sit up and handed me a glass of water. "It's all slipping away," I said, cupping my head in my hands. "Why can't I remember?"

He smiled gently. "Maybe you aren't supposed to bring whatever you experienced back into this world."

I was flinging myself at every option that came my way, no matter how obscure or improbable, and I felt as though my life was spinning out of control.

No more winging it. I needed expert guidance from a medical professional who was trained to work with psychedelics. Not an easy ask. After more online digging, however, I stumbled across a YouTube video featuring a local physician, Dr. Stuart Enright, discussing "psychedelic therapies" and the promise of psilocybin in treating patients with TBIs.

Bingo!

On his website, Dr. Enright wrote that he was "a pioneer in unlocking the mysteries of the brain." Feeling a flutter of hope, I sent him a request for a consultation. The next morning, he responded that he was accepting new patients and included an extensive intake form. For the thousandth time over three decades, I wondered why there wasn't a universal medical history document labeled "Please see attached PDF."

Dr. Enright's office in a renovated Victorian was also home to other tenants in the wellness business, including counselors and massage therapists. The receptionist pointed me to a seat in the small waiting room, which featured the same décor used by the many practitioners I'd seen over the years—pastel wall art, a dusty fiddle-leaf fig tree in a corner, meditative sitar music, and the inevitable Buddha.

It wasn't until fifteen minutes after our appointment time that Dr. Enright, a bald, diminutive man in his fifties, finally walked through the door.

"Be right with you!" he called as I stood to greet him.

Wearing a sweater vest, a large backpack, and chunky silver jewelry on his fingers and draped around his neck, he looked like a cross between a college student and an aging guru. He walked past me to a table with an electric tea kettle and a basket of assorted herbal teas.

"Would you like a cup?" he asked, casually flipping through the tea bags. He had the unrushed vibe of someone who'd just risen from his meditation pillow.

"No, thanks," I said impatiently, eager to start our consultation. My bed was calling.

Tea in hand, Dr. Enright ambled down the hallway, pausing to turn on the lights of his office, which was a miniature version of the waiting room. I followed, trying not to step on his heels in my rush to begin. He settled into the sheepskin-covered chair behind his desk, and I sat down across from him. He proceeded to extract a series of items from his backpack, moving glacially, as if he were practicing tai chi: Laptop. Cellphone. Notebook. Pen. Water bottle. He positioned each item just so on the table, never looking at me or uttering a word.

Breathe, Diana, just breathe. Maybe fussy precision is a good thing. Maybe he'll be this methodical when it comes to figuring out a solution for my case.

He pulled his laptop onto his knees and looked back and forth between his computer and his phone.

"I'm studying your astrological chart," he said.

I furrowed my brow. *Excuse me?*

He set his phone down and looked at my face for the first time. "I did your chart, and your life will be good!" he announced, smiling brightly.

"And just how do we get there?" I asked, my voice tight.

"That's the million-dollar question."

Dr. Enright related his astrological findings in a slow, nasal monotone: I'd been frustrated as a kid (not really), I had an older sister (zero for two), and I took everything too seriously.

I've entered the seventh circle of hell.

I dug my nails into the palms of my hands. We'd already wasted fifteen minutes.

As he placed his laptop on the desk and began to shuffle his papers, I leaned forward, resisting the urge to sweep my hand across his desk and send the papers flying.

"So, am I a good candidate for psilocybin?" I asked in a too-loud voice.

His gaze wavered a bit, and he gave me a weak smile. "Well, we really don't know how the brain works. We used to think it was a separate organ that was connected to the rest of the body through the nervous system. We're only just now beginning to understand how intricate our bodies are."

None of this was news.

"Yes, I understand," I said sharply. I cleared my throat and tried to get the conversation back on the rails. "I watched your YouTube video about psychedelics and TBI. Given my medical history, do you think they could help me?"

Instead of answering my question, Dr. Enright launched into a lecture about the hippocampus, thalamus, amygdala, and prefrontal cortices. "Psychedelics interfere with the thalamus's filtering operation, allowing more sensory signals to reach the cortex. The thalamus is located near the center of the brain, between the . . ."

I'd had enough. "I'm familiar with the parts of the brain," I interrupted. "Let's talk about *my* brain, specifically. Tell me about your experience treating patients with psilocybin."

He looked down at his desk and picked up his pen, then put it down again. "In California, we're still waiting for a law that will allow us to use psychedelics to treat patients."

I took a deep breath. "Yes, I know, but in your YouTube video, you discuss using it with patients. You talked about positive outcomes."

He pressed his lips together and shook his head sadly. "It's not approved by the FDA for clinical use yet. That could be years off still."

My heart sank; this was the definition of crazy-making. *Is he being evasive because he suspects I'm an undercover cop?*

"But there *must* be doctors using it to help people like me," I implored, unwilling to accept he had nothing to offer me.

"There might be a few in Berkeley, but they jeopardize their medical license if they do."

"Perhaps you could refer me to someone? It's fine if they're in Berkeley."

His face lit up, as if he'd thought of someone. But all he did was ask, "May I check your pulse?"

I grudgingly slid my arm across the desk and turned it over to expose my wrist. He pressed my skin with pointy fingertips.

"I think you'd benefit from a cleanse," he said, withdrawing his hand. "There's a well-known ayurvedic treatment center in New Mexico. They'll have you drink castor oil and ghee for a liver cleanse. It may make you vomit for a few days, but the combination restores balance and energy flow."

I stared at him, blinking slowly. A hard pressure began to build in my chest: rage.

What a load of crap.

My eyes darted to the clock on the wall—we had ten minutes left—but I knew I had to get out of that room; I had to get away from him. I snatched up my purse and put it on my lap, opening it to fish out my wallet.

"Looks like our time is up," I said curtly. "What's your fee?"

"Normally it would be six hundred," he answered, "but since we didn't use the full hour, five hundred is fine."

Five hundred dollars? I jumped to my feet, knocking the chair backwards.

"There's no goddamn way I'm going to pay one red cent for this bullshit! You should be ashamed of yourself!"

He stared at me, mouth agape. I grabbed my coat and marched out.

By the time I got to the street, I was shaking. In all these years, I'd never confronted a doctor like that. I'd learned to mask my frustration, to always be deferential and willing to trust. But now I was done with being polite. It felt good to let it rip.

I returned to Dr. Kurtz. Though he'd yet to find a treatment that offered lasting relief, I had nowhere else to go. I didn't tell him that I'd dabbled in psychedelics; I was pretty sure he wouldn't approve. Although he'd clearly run out of ideas—he ordered the same lab tests, prescribed the same supplements, suggested the same treatments—I kept pushing him: "What's the plan? What are we looking for now? What are we trying to rule out?"

"I'm sorry Dr. Greenway's ocular therapies didn't work out," he said one day over Zoom. "I know you had work done on your house, but maybe they didn't get all the mold out. Maybe you should test it again."

"Maybe I should just tear down my house and build a new one," I said, not bothering to mask my sarcasm.

"Or maybe there's mold in your car," he continued, as if he hadn't heard me. "Have you gotten that checked?"

I had, actually; it was clean as a whistle.

Dr. Kurtz was so insistent that mold was the culprit that I agreed to yet another blood panel for mycotoxins. I had no energy left to argue, and though I doubted the test would show anything, I had to keep moving forward. I had to keep trying.

The next morning, I lugged myself out of bed and pulled on my usual outfit of leggings, a gray t-shirt, and a navy puffer. The lab was a forty-minute drive. Although I'd been there many times before, this time I needed Siri to navigate.

The building, a shiny modern box, was located in a business park. I followed the instructions posted on the door and pulled on a mask before entering the reception area. "I'm here for a blood draw," I told the woman behind the front desk. My voice was raspy with exhaustion.

"Name?" she asked, studying her computer screen. She looked to be in her early twenties, with long platinum hair and hot pink acrylic nails.

"Diana Williams. My doctor sent me over for a mold panel."

Her nails clacked on the keyboard. A fist-sized pink teddy bear holding a red heart with the words "I Love You" written in cursive sat next to her monitor. I'd forgotten that Valentine's Day was the next day.

"Ah, he must not have known that we only do the special mold panels every other Wednesday before noon," she said. "I can squeeze you in at the end of March if you'd like."

"That's more than a month away!"

I fought the urge to laugh. *Of course it couldn't be easy, not even once. It never is.*

The receptionist looked up with an expression of utter boredom. She lifted a clawed hand to her mouth to suppress a yawn, then went back to drumming her nails against the keys. I wanted to reach out and slap her, but I didn't have the energy.

I turned on my heel and slammed my way out the glass door.

Once back in the cocoon of my car, I banged my head against the steering wheel and screamed and howled until I was hoarse. Then I cried, deep shuddering sobs that held the weight and pain of thirty years of increasingly debilitating illness. Of chasing a cure but getting nowhere. Of waiting and longing. Of dashed hopes and crushed dreams.

My tears gave voice to the misery and heartache of endless doctors' appointments, the years of misdiagnoses, the futile treatments, the ups and downs. The endless intake forms, the hundreds of needle jabs, the outrageous bills. I cried about falling for charlatans, and about decades of doing everything right and everything possible to feel well again. About pretending to be okay.

I was done. Done with it all.

When I arrived home, I sat in the driveway for several minutes, staring at my house and trying to gather my thoughts. I could hear Alice barking on the other side of the door and the chickens clucking in their coop.

My phone chimed in its dashboard holder. It was a reminder of my next appointment with Dr. Kurtz. I snatched it up and tapped his office number.

"I'm canceling Friday's appointment with Dr. Kurtz," I told his scheduler.

"Alrighty," she said chirpily. "Then we'll see you at your next regular appointment in two weeks."

"Actually, I want to cancel all my future appointments."

"Ohhhh . . ." Her voice faltered. "Well, I hope everything's okay. You know where to find us, so give a call if you'd like to reschedule."

I hung up and shoved the phone deep into my purse. I was calling the shots now.

Alice, now frantic, was barking louder. When I opened the door, I bent down to kiss the tip of her wet nose. She followed me to the living room and jumped up to snuggle when I dropped down onto the sofa. Overwhelmed and spent, I curled myself over my knees and held my head in my hands.

What did I just do?

My memory lapses were getting worse, and not just the short-term gaps, like forgetting the route to the post office. Increasingly, I noticed sizeable holes in my long-term recall. Childhood memories were beginning to vanish. When Mack mentioned people and funny moments from our youth, I could remember only snippets: the time we ran away, stealing a loaf of Wonder Bread as our only provision; our babysitter, a hippie named Dreama; our grandmother's neon-green Ford Mustang Mach 1.

How could I have forgotten so much?

Similarly, I often drew a blank when friends brought up memories of parties and vacations. If I recalled the events at all, they were fuzzy, like old Polaroids fading around the edges. I'd smile and nod and pretend to remember, but I felt as if I were slowly being erased. What was causing my memory loss? Maybe it was the long-term effects of too many electroconvulsive therapy sessions. Maybe it was the TBI after being hit by the car. Maybe it was chronic inflammation from my damaged immune system. Or maybe it was all the above. I'd never know for certain.

I imagined an increasingly dismal future in which my symptoms steadily worsened, depriving me of most things that once gave me joy. At some point, I'd be completely housebound. My mind ping-ponged from one bleak scenario to the next.

I took a few deep swigs of NyQuil to knock myself out and fell into bed.

The next morning, I woke up disoriented, and not just because of the NyQuil. For years, managing my health had lent a structure to my days—juggling appointments, timing supplements, following up on lab reports, researching treatments, dashing out to the pharmacy.

Now what?

Wandering into my kitchen, I took in the dozens of bottles of supplements lined up in alphabetical order on the counter.

No more.

I swept them into a grocery bag and stuffed it in a cabinet.

I made myself a cup of black tea, toasted a bagel, and sat down at the table. I didn't know what to do with myself. Although it was February, spring was just beginning in the Bay Area—the sky outside my window was a robin's egg blue. My house was just around the corner from the Sun Trail, a popular path I'd walked hundreds of times.

That's exactly what I need right now.

I pulled on a sweatshirt and snapped Alice's leash onto her collar.

The hillsides teemed with wildflowers—brilliant orange poppies, wild purple irises, and sprays of blue lupine. To the west, the Pacific Ocean stretched to the horizon, almost unreal in its beauty. For the first time, however, the splendid display of color failed to move me. I couldn't see past my own misery.

I was relieved there were no other hikers on the trail. I wanted to be alone with my thoughts. I walked slowly toward a large bay tree whose branches arched over the trail. Over the years, I'd become fond of this tree and always gave it a pat as I passed by. Now I wrapped my arms around its trunk, leaning my weight into its mass as I rested my cheek against the rough bark. For the first time in a long while, I felt supported and held. Then came the tears, a mixture of despair and relief.

The question I'd been batting away could no longer be avoided: *Do I want to continue living like this?*

The answer was immediate: *No.*

As I walked home, the setting sun streamed into my face and tears blurred my vision, distorting my view. I felt detached from my body, as if I were watching myself from a distance.

Once you know the truth, you can't unknow it.

Back home, I wandered the house as if for the first time. My laundry was strewn on the couch, waiting to be folded. Dishes were piled in the sink. An orchid languished in the center of the kitchen table. Everything was the same as I'd left it, but everything was entirely different.

March 2022 – December 2022

Even as I went through the motions of getting through the day—making dinner, answering emails, brushing my teeth—I struggled to digest the raw truth of the answer to my question.

I moved through my days in a haze. The realization that I no longer wanted to live could only mean one thing: I'd rather be dead.

How could that be? As living creatures, our biological imperative is to stay alive. We feed our bodies to stay alive; we seek warmth to stay alive; we avoid danger to stay alive. But I hadn't been fully alive in a long time, and I was feeling less and less alive—less "me"—as time marched on.

Three years earlier, I'd fought the impulse to jump off the Golden Gate Bridge. Since then, I'd learned that jumpers sometimes survived their fall only to end up paralyzed. I didn't want to end up as a quadriplegic and become a burden to my family.

One night, exhausted but unable to sleep and plagued with dire thoughts, I staggered to the bathroom and pulled my old prescription medications from the cabinet. *Which would be the best to OD on? How many pills do I need to take?*

I squinted, trying to make out the tiny print on the labels, and started to laugh. *Oh my God. Taking pills is such a clichéd way to go.*

Then I panicked. What if I took a less-than-lethal dose and ended up in a coma? I pushed the lot into the trash basket.

I spent the next morning online, reading about Americans who travel to Mexican pharmacies to buy pentobarbital, a sedative commonly used to euthanize pets. But what was I going to do? Drive alone to Mexico and back home again, swallow a bunch of pills, and have Susanne find me? Unbearable.

I couldn't leave the people I loved to deal with the aftermath of my suicide, to face a lifetime of regrets and painful questions. *Why didn't I see the signs? Why didn't she reach out to me? What could I have done?*

I vaguely recalled laws that offered terminally ill patients medical aid in dying. Doctors in ten states, including California, were permitted to help such patients end their lives using barbiturates. But the patients had to be within six months of death. Clearly, that wasn't my case.

I changed my search term to "legal ways to die." The top result was a suicide hotline phone number, followed by multiple links to suicide prevention websites. But after scrolling down to the bottom of the page, I came across a link to Dignitas, a Swiss nonprofit whose motto is "To live with dignity, to die with dignity," and that offered "physician-assisted suicide" to people who want to die but aren't terminally ill.

Does that really mean what I think it means?

It did. Dignitas was unequivocal in its support of what it considers the "last human right."

My breath caught in my throat. *They're saying it's my* right *to die.*

The Swiss group wasn't pushing one more thing, one more test, one more expensive experiment. They weren't going to send me down a rabbit hole of unproven treatments. Instead, they were offering a safe and supportive place for me to die. I smiled at the bitter irony of it all. After thirty years, it looked like I'd finally get help—to *end* my life. I paced the kitchen, feeling weirdly hopeful at the prospect.

I searched the website for information about the procedure:

First the patient swallows an antiemetic to control nausea, then a lethal dose of pentobarbital. Directly after the medication has been swallowed, the patient is offered either a sweetened beverage or chocolate to remove the unpleasant taste left in the mouth.

That last bit made me smile a little. *My last meal will be chocolate.*

I scrolled through photos of the room where assisted dying takes place. They showed an open space, simply furnished but pleasant. In the corner, next to a window, was a hospital bed with a triangular pull-up bar mounted at the head and a neatly folded comforter at the foot. Opposite the bed was a contemporary white sofa, big enough to accommodate family and friends.

Dignitas requires that people soliciting its services first become members of the organization, so I dutifully filled out an application and wired the required $238 to a bank in Zurich.

I leaned back in my chair and drained my tea, which had gone cold, wondering how long it would take before I'd hear that I could advance to the next step: applying for assisted suicide.

A week later, I received a response; Dignitas had accepted my membership request. The email also included a link to the application for what it called "assisted suicide." The phrasing gave me pause.

Dignitas used the terms "assisted suicide" and "accompanied suicide" interchangeably, but the word "suicide" is loaded with judgment and negative connotations. I preferred the term "assisted dying." Although I *was* going to end my life, I hoped to do so in a carefully considered way that would cause the least amount of pain possible to the people I loved.

The assisted dying application required a biographical sketch, medical history, and summary of the reasons why I wanted to end my life. I spent several hours filling out the forms. When I was done, I sat for a moment, my cursor hovering over the "send" icon. I closed my eyes and clicked my mouse pad. It wasn't until I heard the "email sent" whoosh that I realized I'd been holding my breath. Exhausted, I crawled back into bed, and with Alice at my side, binge-watched *Grey's Anatomy*.

A few days later, on a rainy Saturday afternoon, Susanne stopped by for a visit. I had the fireplace going and the tea kettle on. As rain streamed down the windowpanes, we sat on the sofa in my cozy living room, sipping our tea. She knew I'd stopped pursuing treatments, but she still hoped for a miracle.

I set my cup down and turned to face her. I'd thought this moment through carefully but that didn't make what I had to say any easier.

"Sweetie, you know how much and how long I've suffered. You've been by my side every step of the way." I paused, taking a deep breath. "But I can't do this any longer. I know this will be hard for you to hear, but I've found a place in Switzerland that will help me end my life."

Her eyes widened and her hand flew to her mouth.

"Diana! Oh my God . . . "

We sat in silence. "I feel like I should try to talk you out of it," she finally said, her voice thick with pain. "But I won't. I know what you've been through."

She stared at me, her expression bleak. I reached out my hand and she took it. She sighed. "Tell me about this place in Switzerland."

We stared into the fire, and I gave her the broad strokes of the application process and the procedure, adding that friends and family could accompany me. Susanne twisted her hair around her finger as she struggled to process the news.

"You'll know I'll be there with you, Diana." Her voice broke. "But how will I ever be able to get on the plane to come home without you?"

Her eyes filled with tears, and I reached for her. We held each other and cried as the rain hammered the roof. For the heartbreak of it all. The hopelessness. The finality.

A few days later, Susanne dropped off a journal, its cover decorated with bright orange poppies; she knew I loved them. It was entitled "With You to the End," and on the inside front cover she'd written, "Beyond all ends and all beginnings, my dearest Diana, I love you."

Once I'd told Susanne about my plans, I was stricken with worry: What if my application to Dignitas was rejected? What then?

I was spinning out and needed help. I made an appointment with Elizabeth.

A few days later, nervously perched on the edge of her velvet armchair, I studied her serene face. Elizabeth had been more than a therapist to me over the decades; she'd become a mentor and trusted friend.

"You know I've tried everything to get better," I said quietly. "But now I'm done trying."

She held my eyes for a long moment. "I want to be sure I understand you correctly," she said. "Tell me more."

"I no longer want to live like this," I said, maintaining eye contact. "I'm looking into ways to end my life."

Her eyes searched my face, and I knew she was choosing her next words carefully. She was trained to talk patients down from suicidal thoughts, not guide them through the process.

"Over the many years I've known you," she said, "I've seen both your determination and your struggles, and I hear how unbearable this has become for you."

She paused. "Do you want me to talk you out of this?"

"No," I replied evenly. "I don't."

Elizabeth placed her palms together, her fingertips grazing her lips. "This is difficult for me to hear, but I respect your decision."

She drummed her fingers lightly on her lower lip. "Before we get into the details, let me think about how to move forward. I'm ethically and legally required to alert authorities if a client has a plan to harm herself. I could lose my license if I don't."

She thought a moment. "How about this: I'll continue working with you in my capacity as a Buddhist chaplain—on an unpaid basis—for as long as you need me."

Hearing that, I began to cry, and she enfolded me in her arms. I felt a deep sense of relief. I'd made the most difficult decision of my life, and she was going to be with me every step of the way.

For the next almost two years, Elizabeth would help me navigate difficult, unexpected, and conflicting emotions. She also helped me understand that my decision wasn't about quitting. It was about letting go—surrendering.

It took a while, though. "But surrendering means giving up," I blurted out during a session one afternoon. "I don't quit. Ever. I'm not a giver-upper."

I'd always prided myself on being someone who never gave up, who could always find a solution to any problem. And even as I felt increasingly at peace with my decision to die, a nagging voice in my head continued to badger me to keep fighting. After all, almost every discussion of illness and disease comes with a call to battle: Fight to the end! Push on through! Quitting is not an option! Even the Dalai Lama wrote, "No matter what is going on, never give up."

Her face softened. "Diana, surrendering simply means accepting what *is*. Can you accept that you've tried hard enough?"

I nodded, then burst into tears. I wrapped my arms around myself and rocked back and forth in my chair. She was right. I'd tried hard enough. It was time to give myself permission to stop fighting, to accept that, yes, I was done. Surrendering was an act of compassion—for myself.

Unaware of my decision but knowing I was still very sick, my mother texted me a link to a review of *The Invisible Kingdom*, a memoir that details journalist Meghan O'Rourke's struggle with an undefined chronic illness. I devoured the book in a day and spent the next several flipping back and forth through the pages, circling, starring, and underlining passages. It was the first time I'd recognized my own struggles in someone else's story. The obsessive quest to find an answer. The roller coaster of hope and frustration. The isolation. The sheer loneliness of living with a condition no one could see or understand.

Somebody else got it. Got what I was going through. Got *me*.

O'Rourke expressed a sentiment I'd long thought about but never felt comfortable verbalizing: It would be easier for me to have cancer, a recognizable disease that generates empathy and support instead of confusion, judgment, and doubt. Even when I felt awful, I didn't necessarily look awful. Maybe a little tired, maybe a little pale, but more often than not, I was the picture of health. Time and again, people countered my health updates with, "Oh, but you look so good!"

I ordered a dozen copies of *The Invisible Kingdom* to give to family and friends, hoping that O'Rourke's story would help them better understand the complexity and uncertainty of my illness. There would be many difficult conversations in the future about my decision to end my life, and I thought the book might help.

I was especially anxious for Izzy and Nunu to read O'Rourke's memoir. To give the girls as normal a childhood as possible, I'd done my best to downplay the effects of being sick—not just physically but also mentally and emotionally as I felt my essence drain away. Now that they were young adults, I hoped that reading the book would open their eyes to my experience, decision, and perspective, as well as soften the blow of what would be a gut-wrenching shock.

My daughters.

I often broke down when I imagined the toll that losing their mother at such a young age—and under such circumstances—would take. No matter what I did to prepare them, they'd be devastated. They'd have to live with the pain, however they carried it, for the rest of their lives.

April 2022

What are the logistics of winding down a life?

It was surreal, and sometimes paralyzing, to think about, so I launched into project management mode. I knew that getting my life organized was the best way for me to feel in control of what often felt like an out-of-control situation. I opened yet another Excel spreadsheet, this one several pages long and dedicated to my final to-do items: *Cancel magazine subscriptions, update will, close bank accounts, give garage keycode to the girls, plan celebration of life, rehome Alice and the chickens...*

Another spreadsheet helped me organize family treasures I wanted to pass down to my daughters. The list included my engagement ring, my great-grandmother's silver tea set, my great-great-grandfather's 1906 snuff box, sepia-toned photographs of long-gone relatives, and the ribbed gold band my parents had given me for my eighteenth birthday.

Then there was all the stuff of life I'd accumulated over six decades, packed away in dusty boxes on shelves in the storage room—Christmas decorations, tax returns, medical records, ancient sports equipment. I didn't want Izzy and Nunu to carry the burden of sorting through all of it, so I began tackling the job myself. I'd do as much as I could; the rest would fall to them.

Given that the girls were both now on the East Coast, it made sense to sell the house. But it saddened me that the solid foundation of their childhood home would be gone and that a new owner would move in, never knowing the memories it held: visits from grandparents, birthday parties, sleepovers, our family of guinea pigs. All the rich and varied moments that created a textured family life.

My April 15 birthday was laden with irony, and I recalled the well-known quip: "Nothing is certain but death and taxes."

My parents sent a bouquet of spring flowers with a card attached: "To our dear daughter, whose life is a gift." It was a punch to the gut.

How will I ever break the news to them?

To mark my sixty-third birthday, Susanne and I rented a cute Stinson Beach cottage. After checking in, we headed to the shore with our essentials—a pop-up sun shelter, a stack of *People* magazines, and a twelve-pack of Diet Coke. When it grew windy in the late afternoon, we retreated to the cottage's sheltered deck and lounged in Adirondack chairs.

"I want my ashes spread right here on Stinson Beach," I said out of the blue.

Susanne didn't miss a beat. "I'll remind everyone to stay upwind."

Humor became a way through the darkness. When I was on the phone with the rental agent to request an additional night's stay, Susanne interrupted me. "Ask them if they have a hospice rate!" We doubled over with laughter, trying not to pee in our pants, and I had to tell the agent I'd call her back.

Such was the nature of our friendship. We were like an old married couple, so much so that we completed each other's sentences. We shared the same offbeat sense of humor, enjoyed long days at the beach, and loved watching movies on the big screen. On our last night at the cottage, we watched one of our favorite films, *Thelma & Louise*, about two fiercely independent women who live—and die—on their own terms.

After the credits rolled, Susanne disappeared into the kitchen, emerging a few minutes later singing "Happy Birthday" and bearing a homemade, heart-shaped chocolate cake flickering with candles. As I blew them out, I realized I hadn't made a wish and broke down. My dearest wish, the one I'd asked for year after year, hadn't come true—and now never would. I fell into Susanne's arms, weeping, and she rocked me as if I were a child.

May 2022

There was one final document Dignitas needed before my application for assisted dying could be processed: a letter from my doctor detailing my medical history.

Dr. Kurtz hadn't responded to any of my voicemails requesting one. I followed up with a long email assuring him that he didn't need to *agree* with my decision, he just needed to state the facts about my diagnoses and treatments.

After several weeks, he finally replied, insisting on a three-way video conference with my psychiatrist before he would write anything. He wanted Dr. Rosen to verify that I had made a rational decision. During the meeting, however, he dominated the conversation, repeatedly suggesting additional treatments. "Maybe your Lyme is active again." "We could try another supplement." "I'd suggest an updated blood panel." Whenever I tried to bring the conversation around to the required report, he'd talk over me, pushing yet another test or remedy.

Finally, Dr. Rosen was compelled to intervene. "Dr. Kurtz, you requested this call to determine if Diana is mentally capable of making this decision. I'm here to tell you that she is. You don't appear to be hearing her. She doesn't want to try anything else, and she's made up her mind."

By the end of the call, Dr. Kurtz had begrudgingly agreed to write the letter. The last thing he said before hanging up was, "You know, your house could still be a mold pit."

I bit back the expletives seething on the tip of my tongue; I still needed his letter to move forward with my choice.

Three weeks later, it finally arrived. After I'd forwarded the letter to Dignitas, the coordinator contacted me to say it could take several months to review the application materials to make sure everything I'd submitted complied with Swiss law.

There was nothing to do but wait.

June 2022

I'd scattered poppy seeds around my front yard the previous fall, hoping that even a few might grow. I was delighted when an orange field sprang from the bare soil. Dozens of cheerful blossoms greeted me along the path to my driveway. I bent to peer into their exquisite little faces; their beauty was transcendent.

Even after I'd snipped a handful of stems and arranged the blossoms in a vase above my kitchen sink, the petals somehow knew to close at dusk. It struck me as miraculous that, even when cut, the change in light told them night was coming and that it was time to sleep. It seemed nature had the same message for me as well.

July 2022

Izzy flew in from Boston to celebrate her twenty-fourth birthday. Nunu was already home for the summer, and I'd booked a spa weekend in Calistoga for the three of us. We soaked in mineral water heated by thermal geysers and played croquet, a family favorite. Despite the relaxing environment, I was acutely aware of living with a secret. I'd decided to wait to tell the girls until after I'd received final approval from Dignitas. I didn't know how long that would take, but in the meantime, I felt an urgency to create happy moments with the two of them, hoping good memories would help buoy them against a future undertow of grief.

Early one morning, Susanne FaceTimed me from her bed to tell me about a vivid dream she'd had. She'd dreamt we were in heaven. Her back was to me, and I'd called her name. As she turned around, I lifted my left arm to show her a butterfly tattoo.

We took this as a sign: It was time to get our first tattoos, something we'd talked about doing for years. We used markers to sketch butterflies at my kitchen table and took them to a tattoo studio in San Francisco. As the artist traced the butterfly on my left forearm in shades of blue and green, I squeezed Susanne's hand. When it was her turn, she held mine as her butterfly took form on her right triceps.

In the coming months, I'd add several more tattoos. A California poppy on my right ankle. A series of symbols on the inside of my right wrist—☆ x ∞—shorthand for what I've always told my daughters: "I love you more than all the stars in the sky times infinity." A daffodil for my mother, who'd always given me a bouquet of them on my spring birthday. "Edelweiss" for my father, who sang me to sleep with the song when I was a colicky baby.

I wanted permanent messages tattooed on my impermanent body. When I felt anxious and alone, I could look at them and remind myself that I was loved and that I had loved in return.

August 2022

I was getting sicker, and there were days when bone-crushing fatigue kept me from leaving the house. A trip to the market, once an unremarkable outing, now felt like an epic journey.

I had to let go of the pottery class where I'd spent so many hours trying to distract myself by creating objects of beauty. It had been satisfying to shape clay into something recognizable—a glazed vase or bowl—that I'd proudly give to friends. But I'd lost the strength to knead and wedge the clay. I abandoned my box of tools in my studio cubby and never returned.

I also let go of Prison to Employment Connection, my San Quentin program. For the past few years, I'd been struggling to manage the daily operations, and after teaching the class each week, I'd get home and crumple with exhaustion. Too many things were starting to fall through the cracks. Emails piled up in my inbox, I lost my train of thought in the middle of lectures, and I no longer had the energy to pursue fresh job leads on behalf of my students. As much as I hated the idea, it was time for someone to replace me.

It didn't take long to find someone I could trust with my "baby," but handing over the reins of a program I'd developed and nurtured for almost a decade was wrenching. As I trained the new director to lead the class, I often had to restrain myself from jumping up to take over, though I wasn't always successful.

When the metal gates clanged behind me as I exited the prison for the last time, I felt a mixture of deep sorrow at leaving and immense pride that the program would continue as part of my legacy. I was honored to have worked with more than three hundred inmates as they honed their skills, transformed into job-ready citizens, and grew more confident and hopeful about their futures.

Letting go of people who weren't close friends was easier. I found it impossible to make small talk, and I didn't have the energy or desire to discuss my life—much less my death—with anyone other than those closest to me; everyone else would just have to find out when I was gone.

Over the years, many of those friends (now mostly acquaintances) had asked if I'd found "gifts" or "meaning" in my long illness. "I'm still looking," I told them, though the question made me cringe; I wondered if maybe I just wasn't spiritual enough to discover the silver lining in my suffering that others appeared to find so easily. I never did find anything that I would call a gift, but looking back, I understand that fear most often drove their urgency for a reassuring answer. It can be frightening to think there might be no meaning in suffering. As they say, bad shit happens to good people all the time.

There was one thing I *was* thrilled to let go of: dietary restrictions! I'd been on a series of specialized diets—highly limited and universally unappealing—for decades, and now I threw myself into eating whatever the hell I wanted. For ten nights in a row, I devoured a quart of mint chocolate chip ice cream. I regularly scarfed down M&Ms, Junior Mints, and Milk Duds and loaded up on pasta and bagels slathered with cream cheese, washing everything down with Diet Coke, another old favorite.

Vegetables be damned—I never liked you anyway.

Although I couldn't taste much, I still appreciated sensation and texture, and eating once-forbidden foods was particularly satisfying after having choked down countless meals of stringy, high-fiber greens; dry, gluten-free bread; and kale smoothies. I regularly retreated to bed at night with a bowl of macaroni and cheese, and fried bacon up in the morning just for the greasy, crispy, salty thrill of it.

September 2022

My phone dinged with a text from Susanne.

I am so pissed and I love you so much

How can you do this?

How can you not do this?

You're an asshole

I love you

I texted her back.

You know I will always be your favorite asshole. I'm so sorry. I love you.

October 2022

I hadn't heard from Dignitas since May, so I emailed asking for an update. A representative wrote back, saying my application was still under review and that it would likely be a couple more months before I heard anything. I couldn't help but worry that they were looking for a reason to deny me.

Now that I didn't have work to distract me, I was more acutely aware of my symptoms. My headaches had always come and gone; now they did more coming than going, and I pounded ever more ibuprofen. When my night sweats kicked in, I changed my pajamas and placed a towel over the wet sheets. To ward off chills, I'd wrap myself in a blanket and huddle on a heating pad.

But there was no relief from the relentless exhaustion. I ate in bed with Alice at my side, binge-watching Netflix until I could no longer keep my eyes open and turned out the light. I all but stopped cooking and either had food delivered or dragged myself to the market to buy a week's worth of prepared meals. I'd always sped by the displays of cut flowers crowding the entryway, but now I bought bouquets of tulips and sunflowers. What used to feel like an extravagance now seemed a necessary gift of beauty.

Despite trying to get outdoors at least once a day, I struggled with how to break up the long hours. Like a drinker trying to hold off until "cocktail hour," I'd check the clock almost furtively, anxious for it to be 6 p.m. so I could give myself permission to crawl back into bed. On days that I had a little more energy, I worked on paring my belongings. I donated boxes of clothing to Goodwill, whittled down my library, recycled appliance warranties and old insurance papers, and hauled board games, office supplies, and house plants down my driveway, leaving them in a box on the side of the road next to a sign that read, "Please take to a good home."

In the back of my bedroom closet, I discovered dozens of old journals. When I was eight, my mother had given me a diary secured with a tiny lock. I'd written in it every day, addressing neatly penned notes in loopy cursive to "Dear Diary" and diligently recording who sat next to me at lunch (and who didn't), the particulars of my first crush, and my grousing that my brother got to sit in the front seat when we went out for ice cream.

The tone of the reports changed over the years, with my teenage entries becoming increasingly reflective. Looking back, I see the beginning threads of who I eventually became as an adult. Even then, I longed for experiences that gave me a sense of connection, meaning, and purpose, and struggled to navigate those that didn't.

Starting in my mid-thirties, health concerns consumed many of the pages. Descriptions of my erratic symptoms were followed weeks or months later by exultant entries in which I reveled in the belief that I'd finally found a cure. Such cycles of hope and despair cast a long shadow that only lengthened with time.

A journal entry from 2021 reads, "I feel like the life has been sucked out of my body. There's no sign of me anymore. I am so worn down by this and don't think I can endure much more. I beg God for help and still have no relief. Too much suffering."

November 2022

On one of my trips to the grocery store, I noticed a flyer for a "Death Café" on the bulletin board that read, "Join like-minded individuals sharing feelings and exploring questions related to death and dying in a facilitated group setting."

I didn't have the energy to drag myself to an in-person meeting, but when I got home, I googled "death café" and discovered a large death-positive movement. There were hundreds of such cafés across the globe that met in person or over Zoom to openly discuss a subject that, to my mind, is tragically taboo in our culture.

After joining a random Zoom meeting of about a dozen middle-aged and older people, I quickly learned there was no agenda. Instead, people jumped in on any number of topics whenever they felt moved to do so. A woman who'd recently sat at her mother's deathbed wanted to know what others thought about the possibility of an afterlife; an elderly man considering a green burial asked for input; a "death doula" chimed in about the importance of supporting people who were facing death.

Nobody mentioned assisted dying.

The next time I joined the group, I worked up the courage to share my decision to end my life. A few people asked thoughtful questions about Dignitas, and one woman told me I was "brave," but nobody challenged me or tried to make me change my mind. I felt respected and supported. For the rest of the session, we talked about how death had become so sterile and medicalized in our culture—so separate from the rest of our lives.

After we'd signed off, I thought about a solo trip I'd taken to Nepal in 2000 when Izzy was a toddler. I'd sat on the steps of Kathmandu's Pashupatinath Temple, Nepal's oldest Hindu site, to witness the open-air cremations. Hinduism doesn't view death as final, but rather as a transitional state, the first step on a journey toward reincarnation. A procession of corpses on bamboo gurneys made its way to the river, where families washed the deceased, wrapped them in orange cloth, and adorned them with marigolds. The bodies were then placed on stone platforms built on the banks of the Bagmati River, which flows into the sacred Ganges. Women wailed as the fire gained ferocity, reducing the bodies to ashes, which were then swept into the river.

The ritual was at once raw, powerful, and beautiful. I hadn't expected to be so moved, even comforted, by the sight of burning bodies. I found myself viscerally drawn to the honesty of the ceremony, of seeing in full, bright light what is most often hidden in Western culture. It occurred to me then—and even more now, twenty-two years later—that we, and particularly those in the medical community, treat death as a failure.

December 2022

When the girls came home for Christmas, I felt an urgency to share nuggets of motherly wisdom: never give someone red carnations (a personal no-no); know where to place the butter knife when you set a table; always pee after sex so you don't get a UTI; and always, always trust your intuition. And just in case I'd left out any details about sex over the years, I gave each of them a vibrator. After tearing off the wrapping paper—and a shocked chorus of "*Mom!*"—they shrieked with laughter.

There were moments when I had to remind myself not to be distracted by anxiety as we watched home movies or baked together. In the back of my mind there always lurked the knowledge that somewhere in Switzerland, a doctor was reviewing my application for assisted dying and would soon make a decision that would have a profound effect on all our lives.

2023

January 2023

The Dignitas email arrived on a cold, foggy morning: "Dear Ms. Williams, please be advised that the medical doctor cooperating with us has just given you the provisional 'green light' for an assisted and risk-free suicide in Switzerland." The email went on to say that I'd need to travel to Zurich to meet with one of their physicians before I could set a date.

This was the moment I'd been waiting for. It wasn't exactly joyful news, but it *was* a relief after almost a full year of being stuck in limbo. I closed my laptop and dragged the soft knitted blanket from the back of the sofa, wrapping it around my shoulders as I stepped outside. The world was a swirl of gray as the fog blew in from the Pacific Ocean, pushing my hair across my face. I sat on my front steps, suspended in time and feeling numb. I watched my chickens scratch and peck at the ground. It was only when the wind picked up that I noticed I was shivering.

February 2023

Talking about ending my life caused Susanne untold pain, but I had to let her know that things were moving forward. We met for breakfast at a local café. The moment she saw me, she knew something was up.

"What's going on, sweetie?" she asked warily, dropping into the chair across from me.

I took a deep breath. "Dignitas approved my application."

She looked down and bit her lip, fighting tears. "How can this be happening?" Her voice broke and she reached across the table for my hand.

We sipped our lattes in silence, trapped in a shared cone of grief. Behind us, a group of teenagers whooped and laughed as they compared images on their cell phones. The contrast between their glee and her anguish was excruciating. Susanne had offered me loving support for twenty years, and now I was going to abandon her. I felt like the shittiest of shitty friends.

It was time to tell Bob. We needed to work together to figure out how and when to tell the girls. I texted him and asked him to come up to the house the following Saturday.

He knew I was in bad shape and that I had stopped all treatments. When he arrived, his clenched jaw told me he knew bad news was coming. We faced each other on the sofa, the one we'd picked out together years before. I told him how grateful I was for his support during the two decades of our marriage; I knew it was hard for him to have a sick wife.

When I said I was going to end my life, he inhaled sharply. "I'm not entirely surprised," he said, taking my hands. "But it's going to take me some time to process this."

We discussed Dignitas and what was going to happen.

"Do you want me with you?" he asked.

His offer touched me. We were no longer married, but our shared history bonded us together.

"Yes, thank you. If the girls decide to go, they will need your support."

Thinking about our daughters, we started to cry and stood to embrace. "I love you," Bob said, kissing the top of my head. "This feels so surreal . . ."

We deliberated about when to tell Izzy and Nunu. How much time should we give them to process the news? Two months? Six months? There was no playbook for any of this, especially since I didn't yet have a date. I was still waiting for the official green light from Dignitas.

When I called Dignitas for guidance, an advisor suggested we give the girls as much time as possible. But with Bob flying back and forth so often to visit his mother, who was having health problems of her own, we decided to wait until May.

March 2023

As I was sorting through a pile of unopened mail, I came across a reminder notice for my annual mammogram.

I snorted. *To hell with that!*

For thirty years, I'd done all the "right" things in my relentless pursuit of good health. No more. There was no way I would ever get another mammogram. Ditto for a dental cleaning, a Pap smear, or a colonoscopy. I was done with all the medical poking and prodding. I wadded the reminder into a tight ball and shoved it into the recycling bin.

I was just getting started. I tossed the sunscreen, threw away my retainer, and smoked my first cigarette. At Whole Foods, I boosted a ridiculously overpriced bottle of coconut water, grabbing it from the shelf, popping it open, and guzzling it as I exited the store. It was the first time I'd shoplifted since I was a teenager, and I reveled in a heady combination of exhilaration and guilt I hadn't felt in years.

Susanne and I went to a shooting range, where I fired a handgun for the first time. "I want to get arrested before I die," I told Susanne as we drove home. "I want to get shoved into a cop car, taken down to the station, and interrogated under bright lights."

I was in full outlaw mode. What did I have to lose?

"Oh, for the love of God, Diana." Susanne giggled. "Enough with the Thelma-and-Louise bit. That's a terrible idea on so many levels. To begin with, if you have an arrest record, you'll get flagged at the Zurich airport. Then where would you be with your stupid plan to die?"

April 2023

My mother called from Vermont to let me know my ninety-one-year-old father, who'd been declining, was in the hospital. I flew out the next day.

Once there, I watched Dad fade in and out of consciousness and delirium. At one point, I had to hold him back as he tried to climb out of bed, insisting we needed to "circulate," as if we were at a party. I got him settled, but then he began to fret about getting to the airport on time; he said he had a flight to catch. The nursing staff suggested we play along, so we assured him there was plenty of time before his plane left. I later learned that the compulsion to travel is common with dying patients, although I'd never experienced that during my hospice work. It made me wonder if people know, on some level, that they are packing for the last trip they'll ever take.

I needed to play our silly family game one last time. "Tap me, Daddy," I told him. Although it took a great deal of effort, he raised his hand to touch my arm.

"You got me last!" I told him, tears in my eyes. His face opened into the familiar, mischievous grin I so loved.

As the end neared, my mother, my brother, and I stayed at his side, and I played "Edelweiss" on my phone. Over the next couple of hours, his breathing gradually slowed, even stopping for several seconds at a time.

I wanted to be fully present for my father, so I didn't dwell on my own situation. In the back of my mind, however, was the awareness that before much longer, I'd be the one lying in a bed taking my last breaths, my own children at my side.

The pauses between his breaths lengthened until, finally, my father exhaled one last time. In that sacred moment, time seemed to stop. We held each other and wept. It was just a month shy of my parents' sixty-fifth wedding anniversary.

We buried Dad's ashes in a cemetery overlooking the rolling green Vermont hills. As we tossed his favorite candies, Necco wafers and black licorice, on top of his urn, we laughed and cried, imagining how delighted he would be to have his sweets in the afterlife. Upon our return to my parents' home, I was startled to see his wallet on the side table and his shoes lined up by the front door. I felt like a small child again, wondering where my daddy had gone.

Once back in Mill Valley, I felt my father's presence everywhere and in everything I did: as I cheered for his favorite football team; as I twisted his wedding ring—which my mother had pressed into my hand before I left—around my thumb; as I scooped mint chocolate chip ice cream, his favorite, into a bowl with a spoon from his mother's silver collection.

I'd read somewhere that when we exhale, one atom from that breath will end up in the lungs of every other person on the planet within a year's time. I also remember reading that Einstein once said energy can neither be created nor destroyed, and that scientists agree that 97 percent of our bodies are made of stardust. How could we not all be connected? *Of course* my father's presence was everywhere.

I still cried when I thought of the pain my own death would cause, but I'd never felt a moment's doubt about my decision. Feeling my father so strongly, I could only hope that my daughters will also feel my presence after I'm gone and know that my love will always surround them.

May 2023

Spring has always been my favorite time of year, but I'd been dreading this month. It was time to tell the girls my plan.

The biggest hurdle was that they both worked in Boston. Clearly, Bob and I couldn't inform them over FaceTime, but under what pretense could we bring them back to California? "Come home, girls, your mother's dying?"

Not exactly.

Bob called the girls individually and repeated the phrase we'd agreed on: "Mom has medical decisions to make, so please come home." They pressed him for details, but he insisted that we'd discuss everything in person.

A few days later, as I stood on the deck overlooking the driveway, waiting for Bob and the girls to arrive, I felt oddly calm. No matter their reaction, it would be a relief to finally tell them. No matter their reaction, we'd find a way through. I knew I couldn't fully move forward while my daughters remained in the dark.

In forty-five minutes, their lives will change forever.

But then I got a text from Bob: "Stopping for burritos. Girls hungry."

Burritos? I had to laugh.

I considered using the extra time to memorize the letter I'd prepared. But I worried I'd become too emotional and stumble over my words, so I returned to my original plan, which was to read it to them. I needed to stay solid in case they fell apart.

I expected them to burst through the door, upset and demanding explanations. Instead, they strolled in, gave me a hug, and handed me a chicken burrito. I later learned that they weren't as calm as they appeared, and in retrospect, I think their casual attitude was a defense mechanism against what they suspected—correctly—was coming. As we sat around the kitchen table, the girls chatted about nearly missing their flight and Bob's tendency to speed on the freeway. I said little. I felt as if I were hovering above the scene, watching the last moments of an ordinary family meal before a shockwave hit.

I couldn't manage more than a few bites of my food and kept exchanging meaningful looks with Bob. I wanted to get it over with. Finally, the girls balled up their burrito foil wrappers and sat back in their chairs.

"Come upstairs with me?"

Bob stayed in the living room, ready to intervene if anyone bolted. We'd discussed every possible reaction. Would they fall apart? Rage at me? Try to change my mind? I didn't know what to expect, but I was fully prepared to defend my decision by offering to print out stacks of lab reports, put them on the phone with Dignitas, or ask Elizabeth to intervene.

I sat at the head of my bed and patted the mattress on both sides of my legs, inviting them to sit opposite me. The girls looked at me expectantly. I could see they were worried.

I pulled out my letter and began to read, doing my best to keep my voice steady.

My Dear Daughters,

As you know, I've been fighting an illness for almost thirty years. And now my body is unable to recover.

I feel sick much of the time and have very little quality of life. I've tried everything available to help me get better and I've decided there's nothing left for me to do.

I don't recognize myself anymore. My essence is gone.

It's painful to live like this and I don't want to suffer anymore. After much time and reflection, I've made the decision to go to a place that will help me die.

They gasped and I looked up. They'd both started to cry, but I forced myself to read the last sentence, my voice practically a whisper.

I am here to hold, love, and support you until it's time for me to go.

They stared at me in shock, tears sliding down their cheeks. Nunu was the first to speak.

"Is there anything we can do to change your mind?"

"No, sweetie," I said gently. "There isn't."

We lay on the bed together and wept, their bodies curled around mine and their heads on my shoulders.

In time our heartbeats slowed, and our tears ebbed. We wiped our faces, and they headed downstairs to walk Bob to his car. I strained to catch their conversation upon their return to the house, but all I could hear was the clatter of dishes.

During the two days the girls were home, they didn't broach the topic and I didn't press. I had to follow their lead and give them space to process the news at their own pace.

A week later, on Mother's Day, they sent me a bouquet of flowers—no red carnations, of course. The attached card read, "Happy Mother's Day to our deeply beloved mother from her ever-grateful daughters."

Izzy sent a second card: "Please know that even though this will be an extremely tough, painful time, I support whatever you decide to do, and 100% have your back. You have been, and still are, an incredible mom and woman to look up to. Thank you for all your support and love in my life. I love you more than all the stars in the sky times infinity."

I placed the cards on the living room mantel so I could see them throughout the day. I was stunned by the grace of their words but knew that they were only beginning to sort through their feelings.

Just yesterday, it seemed, I'd held them in my arms. Now my little girls had transformed into compassionate young women who were stepping up when I needed them most.

June 2023

I agonized over how to break the news to my eighty-four-year-old mother, who'd lost my father just two months earlier. I was afraid it would destroy her. In choosing to end my life, I'd be upending the natural course of events. Children aren't supposed to die before their parents.

What kind of daughter does that to her mother?

Just as I wanted to protect my children from suffering, I wanted to protect my mother, the woman who'd given me life. She'd weathered my three-year-old temper tantrums and survived my sullen, door-slamming teenage years. She'd patiently taught me to drive a stick shift, using her beloved 1970s-era VW Bug, wincing but never scolding when I ground the gears. She showed me the face of independence by enrolling in Brooklyn College when she was forty and graduating Phi Beta Kappa.

My feelings of guilt over how deeply my decision would hurt her wrestled with the reality that I owed her the truth. I decided to wait. She was still grieving my father, and waiting would shorten the time she would have to bear the knowledge.

When I told my brother, Mack, over FaceTime, he studied me carefully before answering. Other than my mother, there was no one on earth I'd known longer, and my heart ached for him.

"I don't want you to do this, Diana, but you're my sister. You know I'll always be here for you, no matter what."

We spent more time on the phone than we had in years, catching up on our lives and reminiscing about childhood pranks, with him filling in the gaps in my memory. He reminded me of the Christmas when I was seven and he was five, and we stuffed our mother's cigarettes in a large ball ornament—one of many that opened—and hung it on the tree. When we finally fessed up and told her where they were, neither of us could remember where we'd tucked the ornament.

I loved that he was able to make me laugh, even on my worst days.

I assumed Mack would want to accompany me to Dignitas; in fact, it never occurred to me that he wouldn't. But when I brought up flight schedules, he was noncommittal. When I pushed, he told me he wasn't sure he wanted to be there.

Wow. My own brother?

I felt angry and abandoned. What happened to "You know I'll always be here for you, no matter what"?

We danced around the subject during subsequent calls. He was more reserved, and the weight of what was left unsaid hung in the air. In a moment of calm, I picked up the phone and broached the subject head-on.

"Why wouldn't you want come with me to Switzerland?"

Mack had been a first responder for thirty years and was haunted by memories of violence and death, traumatic images that were exacerbated by his near-photographic memory. "I want to remember you as you were," he explained. "I have to stick with the happy memories, or I'll be swallowed whole."

We had differing needs, and those needs clashed. But as he spoke with vulnerability, which took guts, I began to understand his perspective—he was telling me what was true for him. He listened to me, too, acknowledging my feelings of hurt and abandonment.

By the end of the call, something had changed. Just as I was doing what was right for me, Mack was doing what was right for him, and that was okay. I no longer needed him to travel with me to Zurich; he would be with me regardless.

He called me later to say he'd name his next sailboat after me, and that she would always set a straight course.

Other than Susanne and Kim, I'd yet to tell other friends. It was a delicate balance; I wanted and needed their support, but I wasn't prepared to be caught in the storm of inevitable emotion. Or the desert of potential abandonment.

Some friends knew more about my health crisis than others, so I started there, filling in details as needed before dropping my news. Many responded with compassion, understanding, and unwavering support. Others acknowledged my right to end my life, even if they didn't condone my decision. Still others pushed back, imploring me to reconsider, try another treatment, or make an appointment with someone they swore was a "miracle worker." I understood that reaction. I've always been a doer, a fixer; my quest over the last thirty years was proof of that. There was a time I would have pushed back, too, if the situation were reversed.

A few reacted angrily, perhaps triggered by unresolved feelings about their own losses. One of the first people I called was a friend from high school. She mumbled something about being sorry for my pain and found an excuse to get off the phone. I was disappointed and hurt, but I'd known I'd face a range of reactions, including discomfort and avoidance. I understood she needed time to process her feelings.

I wasn't, however, prepared for what came next. A week after our call, she emailed a bomb. Before accusing me of being cruel, she asked how I could do this to my family. Judgment and disapproval radiated off the page. I spent days carefully crafting a point-by-point response to her email, detailing every treatment, drug, and supplement I'd tried, and even attaching medical records. Once I had compiled what felt like my full medical history, I hit send. She didn't respond, so I sent a text to confirm that she'd received my message. I never heard from her again.

She wasn't the only person to respond like this, but given our years of deep friendship, her rejection stung more than anyone else's. In retrospect, I regret spending so much time and effort trying to change her mind. I was desperate to convince her of the validity of my decision. If I could get her see to the light, then maybe I'd never have to face anyone's judgment again.

After a while, though, I realized it wasn't my job to defend my choice—to her or anyone else. All I could do was explain the depth of my suffering and hope that they would understand. If people couldn't accept my decision, I had to let it go.

I was deeply grateful for those who gave me room to feel whatever I needed to feel and do whatever I needed to do, asking nothing in return. "I want you to know I love you and support you always and forever," a dear college friend texted not long after the email incident. "If you need anything—someone to hold your hand or make you tea—just call. I'd love to hear your voice but don't want to invade your space."

Another friend wrote that she respected my decision, adding, "I know it was not an easy choice to make. How could it be? I am sad and heartbroken. How could I not be?"

It was exactly the support I needed.

July 2023

Dignitas informed me that they required more paperwork: an advance directive, a copy of my passport, a certified copy of my birth certificate, my divorce decree, dental X-rays, and a form telling them where to send my ashes.

My ashes. Jesus Christ.

I'd already told Susanne that I wanted my ashes scattered at Stinson Beach, one of my favorite places in the world. But having to think about my ashes brought my impending death into sharp focus. I would cease to exist.

What will happen to all my memories? How can it be that nobody will remember the way the scent of Chanel #5 enveloped me as my mother bent to kiss the top of my head on her way out the door? That when I was a child our family had a tradition of smelling our Christmas presents before opening them? Or that Isobel's newborn ear felt like a rose petal between my fingers?

I looked over at my flip-flops, which I'd kicked off by the couch. How was it possible they'd still be there when I was gone? I recalled Elvis's shoes at Graceland and my father's waiting next to the front door after we'd returned from his service.

What is it about a well-worn pair of shoes that so perfectly captures the essence of a person?

Swiss law requires a psychiatrist to meet face-to-face with Dignitas patients in advance of their final appointment. I flew to Zurich so the organization could verify that I'd made a considered decision to die. As I boarded the plane, it was sobering to think that the next time I took this same ten-hour flight, it would be on a one-way ticket.

Other than taking a short walk down the cobblestone streets of the Old City, I had no desire—much less energy—to explore Zurich. I ordered room service and curled up in my hotel room until it was time for my appointment.

The psychiatrist, Dr. Hofer, a stocky man in his fifties, greeted me warmly in English and ushered me into his bright office, a large room with floor-to-ceiling windows and polished parquet floors. As I always did upon meeting a new doctor, I launched into a rundown of my medical history. I was anxious and wanted to convince him that I was a good candidate for Dignitas's services, in case the "green light" could be revoked.

But Dr. Hofer held up a hand. "It's okay, Ms. Williams," he said. "We don't require an explanation of your decision or an account of your treatments. Even if you had decided to forgo every treatment available to you, it is still your right to end your life."

My shoulders sagged, and I buried my face in my hands to hide my tears. I didn't have to explain myself. I didn't have to justify my decision—any decision—to anyone. Not anymore.

August 2023

Swiss law required I meet twice more with Dr. Hofer over a video call before Dignitas could schedule my death date.

"Do you still want to go forward with dying?" he asked each time we met.

"Yes," I replied without hesitation. "I do."

He'd nod slowly, then add, "You can always change your mind, anytime at all—even at the last minute. It's your decision; it's your life."

I appreciated that he offered me an out, but after three decades of increasing debilitation and decreasing quality of life, I was resolute in my decision.

Two weeks later, Dignitas informed me I was cleared to pick a date.

I wanted to wait until after the holidays, so that meant January. As for which day in January, that was easy. I'd always been drawn to the symbolism of the number 1, which represents unity, spiritual awakening, and new beginnings.

I now had a death date: January 11, 2024.

I lived with one foot in this world, the other poised to leave it. I often woke in the middle of the night, stricken with anxiety. Not about the fact that I was soon to die, but about the thousand little things I felt I had to do *before* I died: Was everyone's passport up to date for Switzerland? What about the thousands of photographs on my phone? Who would take care of the peace lily that had graced my kitchen counter for a decade? I'd found a loving home for Alice, but what about my chickens?

I sometimes felt as though my throat were closing, and I'd lie on my back, taking deep breaths to calm down. Other nights I'd reach for my phone to play Wordle or do a crossword puzzle as a form of distraction. I forced myself to stay in bed because I knew that if I got up, I'd just pace the empty house, contemplating my impending nonexistence.

My nonexistence . . . How can that be?

It was impossible to fathom that I wouldn't see the poppies or my camellia bushes bloom in the spring. That I'd never see another birthday or help the girls celebrate theirs. That I wouldn't know who won the 2024 presidential election.

That I wouldn't hold my grandchildren.

And yet . . . My feelings of grief and loss were dwarfed by my increasing desperation to end my suffering.

I knew, without a shadow of a doubt, that I had made the right decision.

September 2023

The girls decided to move back to Mill Valley for my final months. I was determined to make sure our last days didn't play out like an advance funeral procession, so I kept a running list of over-the-top activities we could do together: charter a boat and sail under the Golden Gate Bridge, go hot-air ballooning in Napa, cheer on the 49ers at Levi's Stadium as we munched on soft pretzels.

But even if I had the energy, would any of those forced family outings really be any fun?

I talked to Elizabeth about my compulsive need to make memories for the girls. "What if it's already been enough?" she said. "What if those special moments have already happened? Maybe there's nothing more you need to do for the girls. No matter how many good times you have together, you can't protect them from the pain."

I knew she was right. It was time to stop trying to control their experience. I asked them to help me plan our time together—activities that didn't require much energy and that we'd all enjoy: We dropped by the local dive bar to play pool. We drove to the bowling alley and challenged each other on strikes. We poked around open houses, comparing how we'd remodel the space and competing to guess the sales price (Nunu usually came the closest).

It was here, in the quiet, ordinary moments together, that I felt most at peace. Most connected. Most loved.

We thought about how to spend our last holiday together. The girls always went with Bob to visit his family in Florida over Thanksgiving, so we looked ahead to December and agreed that it would be impossible to pretend that it was Christmas as usual.

What a blessed relief.

We decided to forgo our tradition of exchanging gifts at the house and instead rent a cottage in Stinson Beach, where we'd play games, read, and take walks along the shoreline with Alice.

It was comforting to have the girls home again. At the same time, I was aware of an undercurrent of unease. We'd agreed to sit down, the three of us, once a week in our living room to discuss our feelings, but we never managed to get beyond the surface emotions of grief. As we continued to dance around the topic of my death, I decided it would be a good idea for the three of us to talk to Elizabeth together. It was time to address the elephant in the room.

Elizabeth drew them out with gentle questions. Tearfully, the girls told me things they'd been afraid to say. That it was unfair I was leaving them while they'd be stuck with a lifetime of pain. That I wouldn't be there for major life events—jobs and promotions, budding relationships and breakups, engagements and marriage, the birth of their children. I wouldn't be there for urgent phone calls when someone needed to know her social security number or to jump on FaceTime to share the thrill of finding the perfect thrifted dress. I wouldn't be there to applaud daily Wordle results, check out the latest recipe Nunu found on TikTok, or gush over photos of Harley, Izzy's beloved Goldendoodle. I wouldn't be there to send—or receive—texts reading "☆ x ∞."

They worried about how to respond to people asking why I'd chosen assisted dying. The last thing they wanted was to field intrusive questions—*Why didn't she tell me? Was she just depressed? Did you try to stop her?*—but they knew they'd have to. We worked together to find the right language.

As I listened to my daughters express their feelings, I was awed by their ability to articulate complicated and painful emotions with honesty and vulnerability.

They had been open and honest with me, and now it was my turn. I talked about what it was like to have a chronic illness that nobody could cure, much less understand. About what it was like to make a decision so few could comprehend. About the incredible loneliness. About how I could no longer envision a viable future for myself.

We met each other where we were, and that, in and of itself, was enough.

Even so, it wasn't always easy. I invited the girls to join me for a movie night, only to hear they both had plans. One of them, in fact, would be out of town for a week.

Are you kidding me? I've got twelve weeks left, and . . . you'd rather be with your friends?

It was hard not to feel they'd already moved on.

I brought it up at our next meeting with Elizabeth. She helped me understand that maintaining strong relationships and carving out downtime was critical to their mental health. As with Mack, the girls and I had different needs, and those needs were conflicting. "You're focused on the next twelve weeks and what's ending," she told me. "They're thinking not only about what's ending, but also what's beginning—how to live without you when you're no longer here."

The girls had to keep the pieces of their lives together so that they'd have a place to land when things got even harder.

October 2023

On my desk was a stack of birthday cards—one for each girl for the next several years. Bob had agreed to mail them every year.

What do I write?

I made gifts for them as well, which I left for Bob to give them on their return from Switzerland. On the cover of each white box, I'd collaged photos of me with each of the girls over the years. Inside each box, I'd tucked a necklace with an infinity symbol pendant and a book on grief. They were also receiving a set of pearls. I was leaving Izzy the strand I'd inherited from my mother and had worn during her birth, and I gave Nunu the necklace we'd had made at the pearl market in China when she was a baby.

And while my next trip would be my final journey, and in the end one that I must take alone, I left each of my daughters a world map, paperclipped with a check, to encourage them to travel together.

November 2023

I could put it off no longer. It was time to tell my mother.

Seated next to the window, looking out as the suburbs crowding the bay below gave way to rolling hills, I began to sob, thinking not only of her awaiting me—I hadn't seen her in six months, since my father's memorial—but also knowing that the next time I'd be on a plane headed east, it would be on my way to Switzerland.

What will my news do to her?

I had learned not to predict how anyone would respond, and I wanted to be open to anything my mother needed to express. I owed her that much. My stomach roiled, and I picked at my cuticles until they bled.

Would she cry? Demand to know how I could do this to my girls? Ask how I could even think of ending my life?

I arrived in Vermont late in the evening and went directly to my hotel. The next morning, on the drive to mother's assisted living apartment, it began to snow, small feathers of white dusting the windshield.

Once in the familiar embrace of my mother's arms, I knew there was no room for small talk. I couldn't manage it, and my mother deserved better. I pulled a stool next to her chair and took her hand in mine.

"You know I've been sick for a very long time, and that I have very little quality of life. I came here to tell you that I'm going to a place in Switzerland that will help me end my life."

My mother has a highly developed sense of intuition, and she told me she knew something like this was coming. After asking a few questions about Dignitas and what assisted dying entailed, she cupped my chin and nodded.

"I brought you into this world, and I will be there with you when you leave it."

The relief was overwhelming. Her immediate response was to assure me she'd be there for me until the end, that she'd come with me to Zurich. I'd been prepared to take care of her, but here she was, taking care of me as only a mother could.

We started to cry, and I told her that I had wrestled for months with when to tell her—that I was worried she might be upset that I hadn't told her long ago.

"It's just right, Diana. It's just right."

My mother loves to have something warm around her neck in the winter, and I'd brought her my favorite knitted scarf. I looped it around her neck, carefully tucking the soft edges into her sweater, before getting up to bring her tea. I pulled a random cup from the cabinet and handed it to her. Our eyes caught over the rim, and we grinned. The mug I'd grabbed read, "Keep Calm and Carry On," the World War II motivational British slogan. Soon we were both leaning against the refrigerator, doubled over with laughter.

Once again, humor to the rescue. Laughter helps regulate emotions, and I'd found no better way to diffuse pain. As Meaghan Mobbs, PhD, a clinical psychologist who has researched the effects of stress in times of war, wrote in *Psychology Today*, "Studies demonstrate that in the face of stress, comedy is a more effective coping strategy than seriousness."

Such moments of levity were a welcome respite from the increasingly unbearable pain of what I was leaving behind and knowing how my family would suffer after I was gone.

I wanted to ease the burden on my loved ones as much as possible. To that end, I met with the events planner at Cavallo Point—a hotel set in a national park at the northern end of the Golden Gate Bridge—to arrange my Celebration of Life, which I'd scheduled for two weeks after my death. As we decided on the hors d'oeuvres, flowers, and seating arrangements, it struck me as odd that I felt little emotion. I could have been planning a wedding or a school event.

For years I wore a long teal knit sweater that, to this day, any of my friends would instantly recognize. Susanne came up with the idea of unraveling it thread by thread and tying a strand around each guest's wrist as they arrived.

I leaned against the doorway of the room where my service would be held, imagining how it would look in January, who would be there, and what people would say about me. I wondered how my mother and brother would hold up. How my girls would hold up. I wondered about it all.

December 2023

Friends commented on how calm I seemed, how well I appeared to be handling all that I had to do before leaving for Switzerland. But that was only true of the big things, like organizing my house for sale. It was the small stuff—losing track of my phone, dropping a sauce-filled ladle on the kitchen floor, navigating the logistics of the two-step authentication process—that undid me. It was as if someone pulled a thread, and everything unwound. Grief rolled over me like a wave, and I'd drown in sobs.

Some days I felt numb, as if I were operating on autopilot. Other days, I bounced from grief to rage. In one moment, I'd go from crying at the sight of the wilting houseplants outside the supermarket entrance—feeling their abandonment and mourning that nobody was likely to rescue them—to swearing at Siri for sending a text to the wrong damn person.

The girls helped me empty the storage room, following my lead and hauling a box of Christmas decorations to the top of the road. They also cleared out their rooms, sorting through the memory boxes I'd started when they were in preschool, tossing out art projects from kindergarten but tucking away the baby hats and bedtime storybooks.

The storage boxes lined up against the walls ripped a hole in my defenses. Seeing the girls' rooms devoid of color and personality was wrenching, more painful than packing up my own life. As Megan Devine wrote in *It's OK That You're Not OK: Meeting Grief and Loss in a Culture That Doesn't Understand*, "Every object in your life becomes an artifact, a symbol of the life that used to be and might have been."

How could so much of their lives—of our lives together—fit so neatly into just a few boxes?

I thought it would be best to empty the house before I left for Switzerland, so the girls wouldn't have to spend much time there when they returned. But Isobel let me know it would help them to have something to keep them busy for the two and a half weeks between returning from Zurich and my Celebration of Life service. Although it was hard for me to leave anything undone, I left my clothes hanging in the closet and the books on the shelf for them to donate.

It was time to let go.

On December 11, I stopped counting months and started counting days.

One month from today, I will die.

One evening, while were were at the dinner table, Harley picked up on a distant sound and barked incessantly, ignoring Izzy's commands to be quiet. Nunu shot me one of her signature eyerolls. "When Izzy has kids, they're going to be completely out of control."

"Well, at least I won't be around to see *that*."

Unsure how to respond, the girls glanced at each other hesitantly, before turning to me, eyes wide. I gave them a wry smile and we burst out laughing.

Will we find a way to laugh during our final moments together?

As I write this, I try to imagine those final moments.

I'm wearing my hot pink Route 66 t-shirt. Bouquets of flowers, photographs, and votive candles fill the space. Family and friends surround me.

"These Are Days" by 10,000 Maniacs plays in the background. It's a song I've listened to ten thousand times and whose lyrics remind me how blessed and lucky we are to be touched by the miracles of everyday life. Though I long wished for a different path, I feel profoundly grateful for my life, for the great mystery of it, and for the many loved ones who've walked beside me.

Envisioning the scene, I can't help but wonder what my last words will be.

Maybe it'll be enough to simply say, "I love you."

Diana Williams died on January 11, 2024.

EDELWEISS

ACKNOWLEDGMENTS

To my dear family and friends who guided, loved, and supported me throughout my life:

Arlene—vodka to Dhanurasana; Bob—bestest Papa ever; Chris W.—way beyond funky; Elsbeth—cuppa pinkie promise; Imke—YFA forever; Joanie—eat eggs!; Karin—language of poetry; Kim—what's the frequency?; Linda—blessings on the blossom; Lisa C.—"Iay, ovelay, ouyay"; Lisa S.—there, behind the tree; Mackie—gotcha last; Margaret—WO for us always; Mom—dances with daffodils; Ron—your eyes; Tina—planting the seed.

To Kay Diehl (master of detail), Julia Scheeres (in her red robe), Charlotte Ward (Queen of the Oxford Comma), and Lauren Cuthbert (a five, after all), thank you for your exceptional craft in polishing my story to a high finish.

Will, Nina, and Heather at Amplify Publishing Group, and Amy Rennert, thank you for your care and guidance in making this the best book possible.